DO THE HUSTLE

DO THE HUSTLE

Life Lessons from Studio 54, the Championship Lacrosse Field, and the Boardroom

DON KURZ

DO THE HUSTLE

by Don Kurz

First Edition
Copyright © 2026 by Don Kurz

Published by
Munn Avenue Press
300 Main Street, Ste 21
Madison, NJ 07940
MunnAvenuePress.com

For permission requests, contact MunnAvenuePress.com

Paperback ISBN: 978-1-969679-35-3
Hardcover ISBN: 978-1-969679-36-0

Printed in the United States of America

To my parents, Lorraine and Bob, who taught me how to succeed in the right way

To my wife and soulmate, Noelle

To Bob Farina, an inspiration and incredible friend

CONTENTS

INTRODUCTION
An Invitation

READING THIS BOOK AND FOLLOWING ITS PRINCIPLES WILL LEAD to a happy and fulfilling life. While it took me sixty years, and more ups and downs than an advanced burpee fitness class, I am now living proof of this.

Unfortunately, I made many mistakes and operated with distorted priorities for most of my adult life—making and losing sizable fortunes multiple times, experiencing a painful and expensive divorce, and generally living with a level of angst that was ultimately unproductive and at times highly unpleasant. Don't get me wrong; I lived large in a number of forums, from captaining my high school championship football and lacrosse teams and being elected to its Athletic Hall of Fame, to playing on an NCAA Division 1 national champion lacrosse team, to being in the heart of the disco craze (including losing my senses at iconic clubs like Studio 54). I was honored to be elected by my beloved alma mater, Johns Hopkins University, to two six-year terms on the board of trustees and then an emeritus trustee for life. I have had substantial business success as a partner in a major global consulting firm and multiple entrepreneurial ventures. But the business success formula is available in plenty of other books, from more qualified authorities than I. No, this is about fundamental life lessons that are available to anyone with a keen sense of self-awareness and emotional intelligence.

My sincere hope is that my life lessons will help you, my dear reader, live a happy and fulfilling life no matter the circumstances you find your-self in.

CHAPTER ONE

You Can't Will an Erection

I AM THE PRINCIPAL OWNER AND EXECUTIVE BOARD CHAIR OF A creative company, Omelet, whose rebrand was inspired by a Leonard Cohen lyric: "There is a crack, a crack in everything, / That's how the light gets in."[1]

It would be easy to assume we named it after the old saying, "You can't make an omelet without breaking a few eggs." The reality is that our founding partners launched the agency over a series of breakfast meetings.

In my sixty-plus years trying to decode life's algorithm, I've learned to accept and embrace each of these truths about metaphorical omelets. First, things crack, so find a use for the silver lining. Second, winning means someone is losing—if you're on the broken-egg side, instead of the sunny-side-up side, know when to get out and into a new game. Third, in terms of a schematic of a business or career, be open to the unexpected, and find a good diner so you can always get a great plate of eggs!

I'm very fortunate to mentor young entrepreneurs and professionals joining the corporate world. Just like the process of incubating eggs, I am happy to offer the requisite career advice, management hacks, and leadership dos and don'ts. My background spans management consulting, taking a company public, and starting a hedge fund. On paper, that's impressive to someone just beginning their journey. But I make sure to emphasize the missteps and failures and lack of an overarching plan that took me from one stop to the next. I characterize it as a catalogue of lessons more than mistakes. More lessons mean more wisdom!

When conversations turn to my life beyond my business career, I often see others' eyes light up. That's because I played on an NCAA Division 1 national championship lacrosse team and attended Columbia Business School while moonlighting as a dance instructor and dancing the Hustle at Studio 54. Along the way, I sold 100 million Pokémon toys to Burger King during an eight-week period.

Eyes don't light up because I'm suddenly a hero to those I'm mentoring. Instead, the people with whom I'm sharing my stories suddenly see a world of tangible and diverse possibilities for themselves, that a career can traverse wildly unexpected paths, detours, and outcomes. They realize that the straight line to the top is a myth and that their various life experiences actually count for plenty. They broke some eggs, too, along the way, but the yolk's no longer on them. (Sorry. Couldn't resist.)

They see that success doesn't come only from late nights studying spreadsheets. They hear my story and realize that they, too, can be worth over $50 million on paper one year and then lose their last $4 million the next, because a bunch of banks got reckless betting on mortgage-backed securities. All you can do is laugh and learn! And that's why I'm telling my story in full here. Do you want to read about a straight line to success? Find some other business guy or gal's story. You want to see how you can take a road full of twists and turns to the top? You found the right person. Enjoy!

* * *

At the core of my story is passion. When you're in love with something, you can do amazing things. You can achieve, overcome, outwork, and win. You can push a boulder up a mountain, and when it rolls back down on top of you, you can push it off, start over, and haul it back up. In that way, this book is about the sum of passion and heart equaling resilience. But it's also about knowing it's time to pivot, to move along, to accept the fact that the mountain doesn't like to be summited. Find a new one to climb when your passion wanes.

I want to change metaphors here. It'll sound a little "locker room" at first, but bear with me when I say that *you can't will an erection.*

No, I didn't mean *election.* I'm talking about the biological requirement for males to engage in sexual activity—and not only because my story begins in the sexual revolution of the 1970s!

This piece of wisdom comes from the most memorable class I had in college at Johns Hopkins University, Biosocial Aspects of Human Sexuality. All of us lacrosse jocks took this course as an easy A. Here we were in a huge lecture hall, and a transgender (the term used then was *transsexual*) person stepped up to the podium.

A former Navy officer, she related her struggles living life as a lie. Despite great success serving our country, she'd been faking her gender identity, and it was killing her. Born a male, "he" felt—to "his" core—"he" was actually a *she.* The message presented was about accepting your true self.

"You can't will an erection," the former Navy officer told us. "You're better off following your inclination, trusting your gut instinct. Life is too short to spend it pleasing others, avoiding your true calling. This is the only way to find happiness."

All of us lunkhead lacrosse players in the audience slunk down in our seats suppressing laughter. We looked at each other like, *Did a transsexual sailor really say, 'You can't will an erection' out loud? College is nuts!* And no, we weren't stoned.

The idea that you can't will an erection was something you never heard from your folks, religious counselors, or schoolteachers. Upon reflection, it gave me a lot of perspective. Say your parents want you to be a doctor, but in your gut, you have no interest in medicine. Or you're struggling to be religious because, deep down, you don't believe in God. This principle became more instilled in me as someone who empirically found that out-working others beats outsmarting them.

If I believe in it, if I want it—when I'm passionate about something—I will attempt to *outwork* anyone to get it. To the extent that I have a superpower, this is it. The flip side is recognizing that the thrill is gone when you are no longer feeling it. That's when you let go, accept, and embrace a new path. You can't will an erection, especially when you no longer care about the outcome. It's just as true in the boardroom as in the bedroom. Aldous Huxley said it best, "*The harder we try with the conscious will to do something, the less we shall succeed.*"[2]

What are you doing right now with your life? Ask yourself, *Am I following my passion? Am I still on the path to my most desired outcome, or is it time to move on?* If you are following your passion, you are already achieving some level of success. If not, you're faking it. Like taking a little blue pill before sex. And faking it is not sustainable. Not for long, anyway.

This isn't a "read this now and start a billion-dollar business by the weekend" kind of book. I never understood those books anyway. I mean, if those others are so successful, why are they giving away their secrets? Why invite all that competition?

My goal in this book is to show you how to deal with life's uncertainties and how to overcome being blindsided by an event, whether it's of your own making or something that happened out there. I want to share with you the secret of how to be resilient and how to welcome and embrace change, failure, and even success. As an entrepreneur, you have near-death experiences all the time. You can't get hung up on regrets. It's like the old Jackie Mason bit, where he says, "Every Jew knows a building he could have bought thirty years ago for nine dollars! They'll all tell you, 'You know what that building's worth today? One hundred forty-seven million—they talked me out of it, those sons of bitches.'"

"You'll tell them, 'Why don't you buy something now?'" Mason continues.

"'Now? No! Now it's too late!'"[3]

The bit is comedy gold, but the message is the exact opposite of my message. I'm here to say that it's *never* too late. You can always regroup and find a new way to move forward. Or to return to the original metaphor of this chapter, you can always go out and buy another dozen eggs.

Consider a friend of mine who bought his house in Laguna Beach years ago for only $88,000. Laguna Beach is one of the most beautiful places in the world. It's a town in Southern California that looks like what you expect when you imagine paradise. So in just a few years, the house leaped in value, and he sold it for $800,000, almost a hundred-fold return on investment because he probably only put down 10 percent of the price as a down payment. Sounds great, right?

Well, not so great, because after he sold it, the housing market in SoCal continued to go through the roof. The same house sold, just four years later, for $4 million. He would never have had to work another day in his life, just living off the income from that $4 million. My friend was so upset by the money he left on the table—even after he realized his massive gain—that he got sick and died. It's a true story.

By contrast, the message I'll teach in these pages—*accept and embrace whatever happens*—yields resilience. It keeps you from being bitter about life. It's the fuel to keep going after losing your biggest client, losing a lawsuit, or losing anything you value. This doesn't mean turning Pollyanna and getting stuck in an unrealistic mindset of *Don't worry, they'll change their minds and come back to us.* No, you swallow the bitter pill. *We lost, they switched marketing firms, and the new CEO brought in their own agency.* It's not fair, but that's business.

Ten out of ten business titans will tell you the same thing, that life isn't fair and you have to accept and embrace whatever comes along. Acceptance doesn't mean liking it. Acceptance just means embracing the reality of what happened instead of denying the facts, blaming others, or convincing yourself that you don't have a path forward. In other words, broken eggs and no omelet to show for them. That's reality. Successful people know how to take a punch and get up off the mat.

Yet the media keeps profiling the twenty-six-year-old who sold their dot-com or AI startup, having made a fortune. That person appears to have won easily and quickly at the game of life. In reality, these twenty-somethings are often beset by a lack of confidence. They benefited from a lot of luck. Deep down, they wonder whether they can be just as successful a second time. Yes, they've got money and fame . . . but do they truly believe they can recreate that success in another venture? The answer is often no.

While I admire anyone who becomes successful (if they did it honestly and legitimately), the people I respect the most have endured body blows and then become stronger from the beatings they took. Their journeys weren't an arrow pointing straight up to the sky. They had their ups and downs. And they are better and stronger for what they endured. They have confidence in themselves because they know that whatever happens, they can survive and thrive.

That's the story of my career, and that's what I want to show you in these pages. Not how to win the game of life before you turn thirty, as appealing as that sounds. I want to show you the bruises and scars that come from being "out there" in the business world—taking chances, succeeding, failing, and getting back in the game. What's different about my story is that I learned these lessons in some pretty wild places. These include the lacrosse field, playing for Johns Hopkins (the school with the greatest all-time record in lacrosse), as well as the dance floor, where I did the Hustle with the hottest stars and greatest dancers of the disco era. You're not going to find lessons like these in the typical business book!

*　*　*

Business and life are both about trial and error. Very few of us, with me at the top of the list, are smart enough to overcome everything without making mistakes. Even Steve Jobs got kicked out of his own company! Did you know that? He was fired from Apple by the very CEO he had brought in to run the company! And when he returned, he eventually tried to start up a new kind of retail experience. It's called the Apple Store. You might have heard of it.

Most people don't know that the Apple board of directors fought Jobs relentlessly on the idea of having stores, whether in malls or standalone locations, because another company, Gateway, had failed with its stores. Jobs overcame being fired, and then he overcame the opposition of the Apple board. Apple stores are far and away the most successful retail locations in the history of shopping. Why? Because Jobs never quit.

Accept and embrace . . . and, also, have great timing and luck. Sometimes everything you do works out great, and other times, well, you take your best shot and nothing works out. As they say on Wall Street, *you can't fight the tape*. Once it's trending the other way, you often can't win. It's happened to me plenty of times, but I never quit. I always found a way forward, and that's what I'm going to show you how to do. For a long time, I resisted the ideas I'm sharing with you in these pages.

When it looked like I was going to lose, I would double down. I'd get angry. I'd sue. I'd blame the other guy. I'd have been a lot more successful a lot sooner if I'd known all that I'm going to share with you. So part of this book is about the lessons I've learned that can make you successful. The other part of this book is about showing you what I did wrong, so you can avoid the mistakes I made.

From the lacrosse field to Studio 54, and from the dance floor to the business world, I've won big and I've lost big. For the most part, though, I came out ahead. If you can exit your own startup at age twenty-six, you may not be able to learn much from me. But if you want to learn how to succeed over and over again, while overcoming any obstacle, without having to, dare I say it, will an erection, you've come to the right place.

So let's get going. I'm going to teach you to do the Hustle.

CHAPTER TWO

Whoever Said Life Was Easy or Fair?

YOU KNOW RIGHT AWAY. THE POP, OR THE TEAR. FOR SOME, IT'S A grinding sound as connective tissue separates from bone.

We arrived at Franklin Field for a preseason scrimmage at the University of Pennsylvania. It was the beginning of my junior year season, 1976, and I played for perennial lacrosse powerhouse Johns Hopkins University. I'd filled a key role as a defensive and ground ball "middie" in my first two seasons. Now, for the upcoming season, I'd be called upon to provide more point production and locker-room leadership. It was all going according to plan. Perhaps this was the year I could even earn all-American honors.

I'd been recruited by multiple blue-chip programs: Cornell, Princeton, University of Pennsylvania, and West Point, among others. But playing for Hopkins, the best of the best, was my dream. I was a two-sport standout for my Long Island high school, too small for Division 1 college football, but lightning quick enough to make up for it in lacrosse.

What I lacked in stature—I peaked in college at five feet, eight inches tall, 155 pounds dripping wet—I made up for in hustle. Not just on the field, but off it as well. From attempting to outwork everyone in preparation and getting in shape, to studying everything I could about the game dynamics. *You have five inches on me and fifty pounds? No problem, I'll cut you up in pieces with energy, grit, toughness, and guile.*

My singular focus meant schoolwork took a back seat. Star athletes get attention, respect, and girls. We had a sense of entitlement, for better or worse. My whole identity was based on doing my part to bring the program its first NCAA national title and being a significant contributor to the cause! Hopkins had won a record thirty-five national titles in its illustrious history, but in the NCAA era, with a new playoff system, we had yet to win one.

As the youngest of three boys, I grew up always having something to prove. Anyone in my position needs a competitive drive to avoid getting lost in the shadows cast by brothers doing big things. Combine that with being on the small side among peers, and you get a guy desperate to be seen and heard.

I was fortunate to have athletic ability—exceptional speed in the forty-yard dash and excellent hand-eye coordination. That evened the playing field with guys bigger than me, but I still wasn't satisfied. I needed an edge. I wanted to win, so I learned to outcompete everyone—brothers, teammates, opponents.

With brothers Mitch (left) and Steve (center) in early 2000s

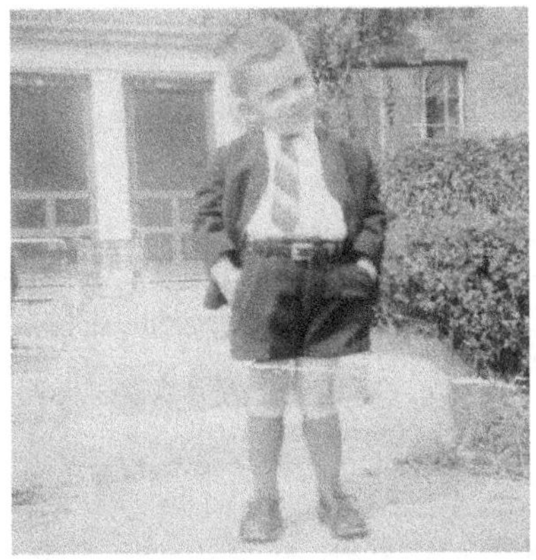

Future mogul? Bayside, Queens, 1959

When I was growing up, there was a television program on Saturdays called *Wide World of Sports*. The opening of each telecast had a dramatic video montage with Jim McKay speaking of "the thrill of victory and the agony of defeat." I took that as gospel. That was my destiny, I believed: to compete and experience that thrill.

We moved from Bayside, Queens, to Elmont, Long Island, when I was five. It was a mere ten-minute drive just across the Nassau County line. I went to public schools. Both my folks grew up very modestly and worked their way from lower class to middle class as my father did better at work. I had a happy childhood. Physicality came easily to me. I wrestled through the tenth grade, often up a weight class or grade level. But team sports were my favorite.

I captained our division champion football and lax teams and earned various conference and Nassau County All-Star accolades. I was voted Outstanding Athlete at Elmont High School my senior year and have been inducted into the Elmont High School Athletic Hall of Fame. I ran with an eclectic group of friends. I was the drummer in a rock group, so I fit in not just with the jocks but with the stoners, too. As a reasonably decent student, I could also hang with the nerdy kids. You couldn't pin me to just one group.

Elmont Football Senior Year

Elmont High School 1972 Championship Lacrosse Team (Number 44; front row, center)

Elmont Football Captains, 1972

Don Kurz
All-League

Elmont Football Senior Year

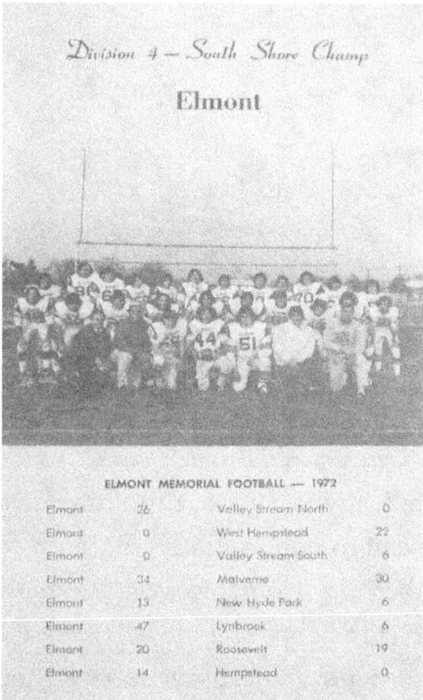

Division 4 — South Shore Champ

Elmont

ELMONT MEMORIAL FOOTBALL — 1972			
Elmont	26	Valley Stream North	0
Elmont	0	West Hempstead	22
Elmont	0	Valley Stream South	6
Elmont	34	Malverne	30
Elmont	13	New Hyde Park	6
Elmont	47	Lynbrook	6
Elmont	20	Roosevelt	19
Elmont	14	Hempstead	0

Elmont High School 1972 Championship Football Team (Number 44; front row, center)

Elmont Lacrosse Senior Year

At my size, college football opportunities were limited, although I did get recruited by schools such as Bucknell and Hofstra. When Johns Hopkins University recruited me to play lacrosse, it was the equivalent of being asked by Notre Dame to play football. I was out of my mind with excitement. During my freshman year, I made an early impression on the field in fall workouts. It was enough to garner the attention I craved as a standout recruit, even after getting arrested and spending a night in a Baltimore city jail. I got into trouble with two other freshmen during a Phi Gamma Delta fraternity rush party for breaking streetlights. (I eventually pledged to the eclectic Beta Theta Pi, unlike most lacrosse players who pledged Phi Gam.)

National Championship Ring

National Championship Memorabilia

When the spring season came along, I was running second-line midfield as a freshman, which is a pretty big deal at a school like Hopkins. (Like hockey, lacrosse midfielders are rotated out with two or three lines playing more or less equally in a game due to the requirement to run up and down the full length of the field.) We won that coveted Division 1 National Championship, which we claimed with a win over our bitter rivals, the University of Maryland Terrapins. It was the school's first NCAA title under the new playoff format. A very big deal for all of us.

1974 NCAA Lacrosse Champions (Number 28; front row, near center)

Ready for breakout year (front)

My sophomore season started out great. I was deployed as a two-way midfielder and had a solid year, measured by playing strong defense and securing the tough ground balls on faceoffs and in unsettled situations. A reporter called us the best team of all time after we blew away previously undefeated Cornell on their home turf. (I don't know what I was thinking when a few of us got caught smoking pot on the bus heading back to Baltimore after the big win, resulting in a one-game suspension. I mean how stupid and irresponsible could I be?)

We went into the last game of the season ranked number one in the country, as well as undefeated and heavy favorites, only to be blown out by our hated rival, Maryland, on their home turf in College Park. Then, just four days later, we were the number one NCAA tournament seed and lost to Washington and Lee in our playoff opener at home. From top to bottom in a flash. The season was suddenly over for the defending national champs.

I worked out hard over the summer and came in hot to "fall ball." The sky was the limit for my junior season. I was committed to being a key part in helping us win another national championship. During the spring preseason, we traveled up to Philadelphia for an early-season scrimmage against the University of Pennsylvania.

Franklin Field is a cavernous, U-shaped, two-tiered stadium that dates back to 1922.

Don Kurz

*Ground ball control
wins lacrosse games*

It's home to Penn's football team, the famous Penn Relays national track and field event, and often the annual Army–Navy football game. At the time, it was also the home field for the NFL's Philadelphia Eagles. In 1969, Franklin Field became the league's first stadium to switch from natural grass to Astroturf.

It was a cold, early February day. A tough day to get warmed up and stay warm when you were rotated out of the game. Before the scrimmage, the training staff gave the players the option to wear special cleats designed for Astroturf. I tried them on for the warmups and absolutely loved them. You could sprint, stop on a dime, and cut at 90-degree angles at full speed. Given that my game was speed and dodging, those cleats were for me.

I had one goal and one assist in the first quarter and was playing well. The cleats on the Astroturf were nirvana. During the second quarter, I was on the defensive side of the field when a Penn player I was covering attempted to dodge about twenty yards in front of the goal. As I was coached, I played up on him and shuffled backward and sideways, covering his various moves. At one point, I had to pivot directions as he suddenly dodged me, switching his lacrosse stick from his right to his left hand (a technique known as "face dodge"). I planted my right leg so I could pivot, and then my opponent rammed into me.

My right cleat was embedded in the turf and didn't give way. Suddenly, I was down on the cold field, holding my right knee in the most intense pain of my life. I heard the notorious pop and tearing sound. The agony of defeat, *Wide World of Sports*-style, but not on TV. Instead, I was living it.

Please God, tell me it's just a sprain! But your gut knows, and I knew in an instant that my season was over.

The docs put me in a full leg cast and crutches for about two months. This was before the broad use of tools like MRI imaging and arthroscopic surgery. (Today I would have had an operation within a few days.) My leg atrophied as the team carried momentum toward the playoffs. By late April, I'd been rehabbing my busted wheel for a few weeks when the trainer cleared me to practice. Coach Ciccarone was anxious to get me back on the field to help bolster our title hopes. I made a few runs, cuts, and stops, and wound up a big shot that found netting and felt my confidence building. I could do this.

I was back.

And then suddenly, another popping sound. My right knee ACL and MCL both tore a second time. I was back in that damned cast and on crutches. Clearly I had returned to the field way too soon.

Damn!!! What a freaking nightmare!!!

I discussed with the coaching staff taking a redshirt year so I could have two years of eligibility left. I was preliminarily accepted to a master's program (with the coaching staff pulling some strings, given my mediocre academic record). This whole episode was a blur, and I just nodded my head to go along with anything the coaches said.

I went home to New York for the summer to recover. I saw a top New York orthopedist to evaluate the merits of a complicated surgery on a young man who was not going to make a living playing lacrosse. In those days, there was no professional lacrosse to speak of, and endorsement opportunities were almost nonexistent. So I was advised that there was no point in going through with the risky surgery. I just had to build up the strength of my bad leg so I could absorb the impact from a contact sport like lacrosse. My spirits were in the toilet.

Once the cast was again removed, I started working for my dad's company. I went from the thrill of competing at the highest levels in the world of lacrosse to working as a merchandiser in supermarkets, supporting Alpo dog food and Glad trash bags. I tried to salvage something out of the summer while I painstakingly rehabbed. While I was pushing dog food and trash bags, I met a young lady who said, "Hey, you want to go to a nightclub downtown?"

She was a dance instructor at a place called New York Hustle, Inc. (You can't make this stuff up.) I couldn't run or train for lacrosse, but I eased into some movements on the dance floor, with her as my guide. Maybe because I was a drummer, I had some rhythm. She said, "Hey, you're really good at this, you could totally teach!"

It was the first positive development in my life since the accident on the Astroturf at Franklin Field.

Now, I wasn't a novice when it came to the new counterculture music scene. In the early 1970s, I got exposed to this new music and club scene emerging in downtown New York, frequented primarily by Black, Latino, and gay folks. I became a member of the Loft and Paradise Garage, underground clubs in Greenwich Village and Soho, that featured incredible music. I fell in love with the beat, the scene, and the people united in a love of freedom on the dance floor.

* * *

Back to the summer and fall of 1976. I was nothing if not primed for a distraction at that point. Before long I mastered the dance move the world would soon know as the Hustle and was nightclub-hopping the circuit just as disco entered the zeitgeist. I returned to campus for my senior year in Baltimore that fall of 1976 with my knee still quite stiff and sore, and therefore was held out of most fall lacrosse practices. But I had developed a new John Travolta–style swagger (though we were still a year out from the *Saturday Night Fever* film release).

The first thing I did was post fliers advertising dance lessons. Hopkins had only recently gone co-ed, and I figured my clientele would be the ladies. (Smart thinking, huh?) I expanded my marketing to include all the nearby women's colleges, including Goucher and Notre Dame of Maryland. It was ten dollars per person for group lessons. We'd have a ball, and I'd walk away with one hundred dollars in cash per hour. And it didn't hurt my social life, either!

I started spinning records at the campus bar, The Rathskeller. The drinking age at the time was eighteen. Nobody else in Baltimore was as hip to the tunes as I was. I dropped the latest extended play-cuts on twelve-inch vinyl. I negotiated a stipend to curate a collection of all the hottest dance material hitting the market. The record store called me every Tuesday and Thursday about the new releases. It was bananas. I was suddenly Disco Donny, the Rathskeller disc jockey. I felt like the cool kid again, not a busted-up jock. Word got around. Someone from Arthur Murray Baltimore approached me after seeing me dance at the Baltimore disco, Casablanca. The conversation went something like this:

"Hey, what are you doing there?"

"I'm dancing! What does it look like I'm doing here?"

"No, what dance is that? Would you like to come teach at Arthur Murray?"

"I'm already teaching."

They made an offer of consistent income no starving student could refuse. Arthur Murray was desperate to get young people in, since no one my age wanted to learn the foxtrot. I was featured in a video for their national program on the new dance craze. I was basically teaching what I'd learned from the girl in Long Island that summer. I added a few moves, making it up as I went along. I was the center of attention and teaching at Arthur Murray three hours a night.

I hobbled through preseason lacrosse in the winter of 1977. My coaches could see that I was tentative, no longer making the sharp cuts at full speed that had been my hallmark. I was likely triggered by what had happened the previous year in Philly and the intense pain of the two ACL/MCL tears within four months. I was playing like crap, and I quickly dropped on the depth chart from one of the top midfielders towards the bottom. Coach Cic kept saying, "You're doing okay, you'll be good. You'll earn your way back into a key role over the next month." But I had my doubts.

One of my student's lesson plans at Arthur Murray

I went through the motions at practice, favoring my gimp knee. When your game is based on speed and agility, you can't afford to lose that edge. A player who is six foot three and 225 pounds might be impacted by a knee problem but can somewhat compensate with power. My gut was telling me I'd never get back to where I was. I knew I would be relegated to the bench. Every morning, I was exhausted from going from classes to practice to teaching dancing at night. My schoolwork, never my top priority to begin with, suffered. Something had to give.

Coach looked at me like I had five heads when I sat down in his office and told him I was trading in my jersey for a polyester Huckapoo shirt to go teach the Hustle at Arthur Murray.

"Disco-dance instructor?" he asked, shocked. "Are you shitting me?"

"Nah, I ain't," I replied, shaking my head like John Travolta in the newly released film *Saturday Night Fever*.

"Nobody quits the Hopkins lacrosse team. Look, Za Za [my nickname on the lax team], you're not playing well, but you'll get there. You are a core part of our plan to win it all this year, and your team needs you out there."

"Sorry, Coach—I've lost that lovin' feeling." Okay, I'm paraphrasing, but you get the point.

Teammates scratched their heads. Some whispered I was coming out of the closet. I ramped up my teaching to five hours a night if only just to fill the hours with something to take my mind off lacrosse. I experienced pangs of regret that linger to this day. But I made the jump and tried not to look back.

* * *

In terms of academics, I wasn't exactly a member of the honors society. I'd been busy with lacrosse and dance, so when I graduated, there weren't a ton of job recruiters knocking down my door. As a hedge, I had applied to Columbia Business School in their MBA program.

My grades and test scores were marginally passable, and with the help of a series of strong interviews with the admissions office, I somehow got accepted to this Ivy League institution. I suffered some workload shock when I went from high school to Hopkins and again when I went from undergrad to grad school. This was especially true because most of my classmates had been out in the workforce gaining experience while I was teaching moves on the dance floor. I was the youngest and most inexperienced (and definitely most immature) student at Columbia Business School.

On the dance floor, however, I made a seamless transition. I was back teaching the Hustle to eager students at Columbia and to their friends across the city. Dan Holmsby was one of my students. He was head of manufacturing for Anne Klein and worked with celebrated fashion designer Donna Karan. Dan loved the nightlife and thought I was the coolest cat in the world. Of course, a top fashion house in New York had a golden ticket to the hottest new discotheque in the world, right? Dan said, "We're going to Studio 54 tonight. You gotta come along!"

This was the fall of 1977, and Studio 54 had opened in April of that year. Regulars included Mick and Bianca Jagger, Jacqueline Kennedy Onassis, Princess Caroline of Monaco, Liza Minnelli, Andy Warhol, Truman Capote, Jack Nicholson, Warren Beatty, Elizabeth Taylor, and many of those famous in the arts, culture, or even politics. (Jimmy Carter's new chief of staff, Hamilton Jordan, had been caught snorting cocaine in one of the private rooms at the club.)

When Dan and I arrived at Studio 54, I couldn't believe the line outside. Back then, no dance club I'd ever seen had lines like that. We walked up to the doorman who waved us in. *Hell, yes,* I thought. Literally thousands of people queued up, loitering outside the velvet rope for glimpses of David Bowie, Cher, Grace Jones, Diana Ross, Elton John, Michael Jackson, or the Queen of Disco herself, Donna Summer. I went frequently enough with the Anne Klein people that before long, I could usually get in on my own. By usually, I mean—with full transparency—that I stood outside plenty of times, waiting like your average schmo.

It was a circus of the world's most famous people, coupled with a bizarre mix of counterculturalism. The club didn't care about letting in the straight rich people. They made so much money it didn't matter. (As it turned out, they didn't pay much in taxes on those earnings, but that's a story for another day.) So as a straight white guy who was not a celebrity, getting admitted was highly unusual.

Disco Donny even made it into the VIP room downstairs where the real shenanigans took place. I can't talk about what I saw down there—too many of the guilty are still walking this Earth. But use your imagination, think about sex and drugs 1970s-style, and you can get a sense of what went on.

I hit another pivot point not much later. I'd spent the first semester at Columbia teaching dancing and club-hopping and rarely made it to class. Just having too much fun, caught in the excitement, in the epicenter of this disco thing that swept across the country. At the holiday break, my old man sat me down and gave me the clearest accounting lesson I ever learned.

"Look, Don, you got these C's and D's and you're out partying all the time teaching this dancing." He shook his head and removed his reading glasses. "What, you expect me to keep paying this tuition and you can't make decent grades? You're gonna teach dancing all your life, Donny?"

I had no answer. We made a deal that I'd pull it together spring semester or I could pay my own way with student loans, or just drop out. His words cut deep. How long could I stay the cool guy with the dance floor moves? Was I really going to make a career working at Arthur Murray teaching the Bump, the Bus Stop, and the Disco Finger with some ballroom waltzes mixed in? Nah, I'd eventually need a new circle to be the center of. And any way you slice it, this would require making serious money.

I was afraid of what was next more than I was in love with the now. It was terrifying to imagine being the thirty-five-year-old high school star player working at the convenience store, still reliving the homecoming game. Even creepier was discovering you're the oldest guy at the nightclub, master of last decade's dance moves, trying to cut out on a bar tab. Yikes. That wasn't for me. "I'm out," I said. I had to get serious. But how?

CHAPTER THREE

Getting Down to Business

I **HIT THE BOOKS AND SUBSTANTIALLY TONED DOWN MY NIGHT** club life. My new mileposts became grinding out the case studies and standing out in business school classes. I flipped the switch from hobby to career, willing to do eighty, a hundred hours—whatever it took—to catch up and pass my classmates. My pain tolerance was remarkable. *Oh yeah, you think you know statistics? I've been up for three days straight. Let's go!*

My grades went up, but my résumé was light on work experience. My interviews for a summer internship went like this:

"Wow, so . . . you won a national championship! Excellent. And you . . . danced . . . (looks up) you taught dancing?"

"Yeah, I was the first college guy on the East Coast to know the Hustle. I got in early."

"Like, the disco dance?"

"Exactly. Studio 54—you heard of it?"

"Of course, it's all over Page Six. So you're a regular Tony Manero."

The recruiters enjoyed my stories of sport and dance triumph but favored applicants who'd been out in the workforce between undergrad and B-school. I settled for a gig at JCPenney. Not in the store, but at corporate headquarters on 6th Avenue and 52nd Street in Manhattan. They were jockeying at the time with Sears for top mass merchandiser. The company started down South before centralizing operations in New York to be close to the apparel industry. Fun fact: A young Sam Walton ran a JCPenney store in Iowa before starting his own superstore chain—Walmart.

I interned in the strategic planning department. They liked what I did and eventually hired me as an assistant to their executive committee. I was de facto chief of staff managing special projects. JCPenney didn't have a lot of MBAs working for them back then, so I was a bit of a novelty. Senior management marveled at my analytical skills and, again, I was the center of attention for being very good at something.

I was recruited away after two years to the consulting firm Coopers & Lybrand (now PricewaterhouseCoopers). This was a rude awakening, to find plenty of folks smarter than I was. I had fallen back to mediocre. I had an extremely tough boss, a South African named John Kneen. Everything I did for him in the first year, he ripped up and made me redo. I slogged through eighty- to ninety-hour weeks trying to get ahead, but he'd throw me more work. Weekends? Forget about it. Vacations? Not a chance.

He could flip the pages of a 200-page deck and find a typo on page 132 within five minutes. I kid you not. (To this day, I will endeavor to never release any document with a typo.) He wasn't the friendliest guy, but we got along well enough, and he became a great mentor. He taught me to write, to present, and to get things perfect. I followed him to Cresap, McCormick and Paget, a management consulting firm roughly the size of McKinsey at the time. I survived a couple of mergers and ultimately ended up running the New York office.

A few years after I started, I was transferred to Los Angeles to launch their financial institution's consulting practice before returning to New York as a senior partner. That company is now Willis Towers Watson—a huge, publicly traded consulting company. I get dizzy just trying to remember all the iterations of names of the companies I've worked for. The main thing is that I got a lot of experience and expertise pivoting through the management consulting profession. I was also burned out.

You could say—and, again, forgive my bluntness—I could no longer will my erection. Time to do something else.

* * *

It was 1990, and I was still in my early thirties and pulling in close to $200,000 a year—a substantial salary today, let alone in 1990. But I wasn't married with kids, so I had the freedom to walk away and find a new passion. I was feeling the entrepreneurial itch and had a buddy doing promotional marketing for fast-food chains. Playing off the McDonald's Happy Meal trend, they secured licenses from Hollywood to make toys for kids' meals. They'd approach Arby's, Wendy's, and Burger King with an idea.

"We own the rights to *Little Mermaid* and can custom-produce for you millions of action figures to market your hamburgers to kids and their parents. We'll make the toys and you'll see a massive bump in sales."

It was a winning proposition for the client, and for me as a next career move. I could always come back to consulting, but for now at least, I needed a breather.

I signed on with Equity Marketing in New York as its executive vice president (absurdly fancy title for a tiny company), took a 50 percent pay cut, and got a little equity. I was just in time for a new licensing deal we were running for a family of bizarre little yellow people. *The Simpsons* had started as a comic strip by Matt Groening in a Los Angeles alternative weekly before being developed for *The Tracey Ullman Show*. After three seasons, Fox Broadcasting gave the concept its own programming slot, and our team got in early to secure the licensing rights.

The Simpsons brand was blowing up into an enormous phenomenon as I joined the company. Soon, we were making a fortune selling these free-with-purchase premiums. What's not to love about the simple value proposition: You buy a kids' meal, you get a free Bart Simpson figurine? We did a ton of tray liners, point of purchase items in stores, and what's called a self-liquidator: When you buy a certain amount of food—say, $3.50 worth—you get a full, life-sized Bart, Homer, Lisa, Marge, or Maggie

Simpson doll for the special price of $3.49. (A similar doll would retail for up to $20 at a toy store.)

The promotions worked and Equity Marketing was raking it in, but as the promotion matured, the franchisees got stuck with all the extra inventory of self-liquidator dolls. For me, it was the worst of all worlds—I didn't participate in the multi-million–dollar profit windfall, as I joined the company too late in the process. Yet, I had to deal with the fallout from our biggest client, Burger King, who was really pissed off at owning all the nonrefundable inventory. The promotion earned about $50 million in revenue for Equity Marketing (equivalent to about $120 million today) with enough profit that the principal owner could retire and never have to work again.

My first task was to deal with all these very pissed off corporate marketing execs and franchise owners threatening to never do business with us again. I and another partner, Stephen Robeck, conceived of a barter deal, an accounting hack really, whereby we took the inventory off their books, and they got credit for discounted future purchases. The accounting ploy was to certify that their future discounts were valued at the same amount as the inventory—something almost impossible to prove.

So we took all the excess dolls back and resold them to carnivals and international outlets—Fox wasn't super happy about that, but grudgingly approved as long as we paid them new royalties on the sales. Equity Marketing also kept the net revenue after paying Fox and the cost of logistics. Meanwhile, we locked Burger King franchise owners into another three-year deal, so they could use their credits as discounts. It was the ultimate win-win! After years of fine-tuning spreadsheets, I got to loosen my tie (actually stopped wearing suits and ties), roll up my sleeves, think on my feet, devise a creative solution, and, along with my partner Stephen, save the company's ass.

Another piece of this story proved fortuitous.

The principal owner had made a ton of money on the Simpsons deal and had gotten a bit complacent. My business partner, Stephen, was already one-third owner of Equity Marketing. With the newly formed three-year sales backlog with Burger King, we initiated a leveraged buy-out of the company, in which we purchased it from the majority partner. Drama and turmoil ensued. It was a real standoff. Our negotiating leverage was to start a new company and walk away, leaving the firm without day-to-day leadership at a precarious moment. At times acrimonious, it took some brinkmanship to get the buyout done.

In another creative twist, we used the company cash and a multiyear note to purchase the company. I compensated Stephen for his existing one-third equity stake with proceeds from future net income of the company. He was paid in full within a few years. We became 50/50 partners and co-CEOs. I remember white-knuckling it up to a family reunion in the Catskills just as the deal closed. A true out-of-body experience as our lawyers from Fulbright and Jaworsky closed the deal while I was in the car heading north from Manhattan.

We grew like a weed from there. My finance background and connections came in handy, and we decided to take the company public on the Nasdaq exchange. We moved our office to LA to be closer to the entertainment business, where much of the licensing was originating. It also helped to be three time zones closer to China, where our toys were made, and to be able to fly direct from LAX to see our Hong Kong office and our mainland Chinese manufacturers. We went public in February of 1994, which happened to be a terrible time for an offering, as the Fed had unexpectedly raised interest rates. Money supplies tightened, and the markets weakened, but we got listed after a few false starts.

The win came with a painful lesson. An old family friend had asked if I needed help finding an underwriter for the deal. He had a connection to a company called Josephthal and offered to make an introduction. At the time, there was no discussion of a fee, and, for context, I make introductions for friends all the time with no expectations of getting paid. It is what friends do for one another—particularly close friends.

Emak IPO Prospectus Memorabilia, 1994

Emak Hong Kong office staff, early 2000s (front row, fourth from right)

I then made a big mistake and said something to the effect of, "If your introduction leads to a deal, I'll take care of you." As fate would have it, that company underwrote our deal (there were several other options for underwriters), and then the family friend revealed—after we selected Josephthal—he was looking for a mid-to-high six-figure sum for a total deal that would raise about $10 million. There would already be over $1 million in fees paid to the underwriter, lawyers, and accountants, so adding another $500,000 plus would make the deal unmarketable.

We met several times and, ultimately, we offered him $50,000 for making this introduction. He found that wholly unacceptable and threatened to do everything possible to hold up the deal unless he was paid his asking price. I fully believed I was helping him by using his connections and paying him a tidy sum that would be equivalent to over $100,000 today. It was very unpleasant. I stood my ground and demanded that the underwriter defend and indemnify the company and its officers and directors if they wanted to go through with the deal. It ended up going to court. He won a verdict that was roughly equivalent to what we had offered him (in the $50,000 range). Of course, he then had to pay about one-third of the award to his attorney, so he likely netted out with less than he would have if there had been no litigation. He then appealed the lower court ruling, but his appeal was denied and the lower court ruling was affirmed. He tried to sue my partner and me personally, but that suit was dismissed. (To add irony to insult, the SEC and Nasdaq limit the total fee payments because they don't want you channeling large sums of money from the public to service providers like attorneys, accountants, finders, and family members.)

I still find this entire episode hard to believe. To this day, I make calls for people all the time. You need an intro? Hang on, check your email. You're welcome. You live and learn. But I never left things fuzzy after that. Dot your i's and cross your t's; leave nothing to chance. Trust me on this. And always document any deal in writing.

I was absolutely wrong not to insist on clarity up front. As a point of fact, he made an introduction to a firm that raised capital for us. That it was done through one phone call rather than months of work is arguably immaterial to the deal. Furthermore, one person's version of what "I'll take care of you" means can differ wildly from another person's. If I had insisted on clarity up front, he could have asked for anything he wanted, and I would have politely declined his intro and used another underwriter. After all, Josephthal was far from Goldman Sachs. If I had listened to my gut, I would have walked away from this deal early on, but I buried the feelings and paid the price. It would not be the last time that I would let my pride and sense of justice overrule making pragmatic decisions.

*　*　*

The company did very well.

EMAK (Equity Marketing's holding company and Nasdaq ticker symbol) debuted at $6 a share, drifted lower for a while with the interest rate pressure, and then reached $30 per share after a couple of years. I owned over 30 percent of the common stock, so my net worth was north of $50 million. In the late '90s, that was quite a sum of money for a dude from Elmont.

I had the opportunity to take some profits off the table a few years after the IPO, with a secondary offering, which is usually a smart thing. Don't get greedy; prepare for a rainy day. Stocks go down as well as up.

NASDAQ 10-year market open milestone, 2004

Bear Stearns approached us with a deal where I (and my partner Stephen) would sell some of our personal holdings, along with the company banking $25 million, and cash out with $5 to $10 million each. I got uncomfortable because I sensed our business was weakening. These offerings take a few months; you go on the road-show, tell everyone things are great, then you turn around and sell stock in the offering. Four months later, your weak projection intuition comes true and the stock tanks. You get lots of ticked-off people and usually you get sued. Some class-action lawyer wrangles you into settling. I got cold feet, so I pulled the offering, preferring to wait until our forecast brightened.

You can convince yourself of anything and, in this case, it was this: *Let me close one more deal and there will be no doubt.* The irony is that no investors thank you for having their back. *Gee, we appreciate your being principled enough to look out for our best interests—here's a medal of honor.*

Nope. They go about their business and sell your company's stock the second it suits them. I didn't want to look people in the eye knowing they might be buying into an offering that would lose money. Queue late '99 and 2000 and I wish I'd been more of a shark. If I had banked $10 million then and put the proceeds into an S&P 500 index fund, it would be worth $100 million today. An episode like this can easily make one quite cynical.

Two bites of reality hit us hard. Everybody knows about the dot-com crash. The internet bubble burst in 1999, proving then Federal Reserve Chairman Alan Greenspan's prescient warning of "irrational exuberance." Who knew? I hadn't succumbed to trying to reposition us as an internet-type company, where many enterprises were getting a big stock boost. Nevertheless, the whole rug got pulled out from under the markets. Sorry, your investment in Broccoli dot.com was now worthless.

The second was Pokémon. We'd done a huge promotion with Burger King, to the tune of more than 100 million toys. That's one toy for every three people in the United States that year, including your ninety-year-old great-grandmother. It was insane. We also sold various collectible self-liquidating items. For eight weeks, we printed money.

Then tragedy hit.

Two infants died by choking on the plastic shell that housed the toy. It's believed the clamshell packaging formed a suction, and if an infant rolled over in the crib, assuming the packaging was left in the crib, they could suffocate. One dead child would have been a tragic anomaly. Two was *turn out the lights*. Our world was turned upside down emotionally and financially. Lawsuits hit, insurance companies ultimately settled, and Burger King—our biggest client—distanced itself from us. The fast-food chain then spun off its warehouse and distribution arm, AmeriServe, which purchased the toys and distributed them to the restaurants. This firm went bankrupt within a year and we were left holding about $25 million in receivables with no recourse to the much bigger Burger King Corporation.

It was an absolute tragedy for the infants and their families, full stop. It was a business disaster for Equity Marketing. Every item we sold, including the Pokémon toys and clamshell packaging, was designed and tested to Burger King's stringent safety specifications—"0 age graded" and deemed safe.

Life isn't fair, and neither is business.

The cruel fact is, the laws of probability have it that if you put 100 million items into every corner of the United States within an eight-week time frame, something bad can very well happen no matter how careful you are.

Time that with getting married for the first time, as I did on February 5, 2000. Everything freezes in bankruptcy, and EMAK was an unsecured creditor. This made planning a wedding and going on a honeymoon, shall we say, interesting. Fortunately, I had a great board of directors who handled the immediate aftermath of the AmeriServe bankruptcy.

We petitioned for preference payments, saying you're not getting any more toys unless you pay us. Burger King deemed us essential, since, if you don't offer any toys with your kids' meals, you're not going to sell many hamburgers and other food for the accompanying adults—Mom will just take them across the street to McDonald's. The court approved a payment schedule so they could keep the franchisees competitive and happy. (Fun fact: The average check that accompanies a kids' meal is three times the size of the average customer check without a kids' meal at fast food companies.)

How many near-death experiences is that? Wait, there's more.

Headwinds continued in biblical proportions. The dot-com hangover begat 9/11 begat Enron begat Worldcom begat Sarbanes-Oxley. A cascade of body blows hit the markets in the early aughts. Some terrible, most criminal, and one a legislative bridge too far.

The events of 9/11 speak for themselves. Markets don't like uncertainty, and the days and weeks following the terrorist attacks were tremors after the big one. Enron collapsed amid gross accounting violations in late 2001, and Worldcom followed six months later. The repercussion for our company was the Sarbanes-Oxley Act of 2002. Our country's leadership had a penchant for overcorrection during the early Bush administration, and this act from Congress was the dictionary definition of unintended consequences.

Sponsored by Sen. Paul Sarbanes (D-MD) and Rep. Michael Oxley (R-OH), the act created strict new rules for accountants, auditors, and corporate officers, and imposed stringent recordkeeping requirements. Your Enrons and Worldcoms should—certainly in hindsight—have these higher standards in place, being large enough entities to absorb the costs. For a small company like EMAK, it meant spending an absurd extra $1 million plus on compliance. That is in addition to the $1 million plus we were already spending to be publicly traded. Just brutal.

Our stock value had been on a nice run until the Pokémon tragedy and the AmeriServe bankruptcy. Sales were over $200 million and EBITDA (a Wall Street proxy for cash flow—meaning "earnings before interest, taxes, depreciation, and amortization") was over $20 million annually. (That's the equivalent of almost $400 million in sales and $40 million in EBITDA today.) After both of those, we became what is often called an orphaned stock. Very few analysts were following us, and without anyone writing research reports, no institutional traders were encouraging their sales forces to push the stock. We became a "trade-by-appointment" company, or a thinly traded stock. Such stocks are highly volatile, since any significant purchase or sale rocks the value like an earthquake. You sell some shares, and the value plummets. You buy some, and the value jumps. There is just not enough weight to keep it in play, as they say. You add Sarbanes-Oxley expenses, and you have to ask: *Why are we a public company? We aren't raising money; what do we do?*

Emak press headshot, 2004

You go private.

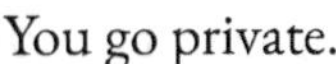

Strauss Zelnick and his private equity team at Zelnick Media were interested in helping us make this pivot. Typically, a private equity group needs an internal manager from the company to back and run the operation once the deal closes. Since I owned a third of the stock and believed in the long-term value of the company, I agreed to support the proposal. They sent a letter to our board pitching a go-private transaction.

"We've talked to Don, and he's backing the idea and offered to run the new operation."

Well, some members of the board were very unhappy. "Don, you went around our backs. You're trying to steal the company."

"No, I didn't—it's the best thing for the company. Shareholders will get a nice premium to the current stock price and get immediate liquidity. Right now, shareholders are trapped in an illiquid stock, so we are giving them a great option."

After a few weeks of behind-the-scenes drama, I got fired.

It was a boardroom coup, and I was out. That's how it works sometimes. You choose a path, make the decision, stick your neck out, and get whacked. The reason—if we're getting granular—stems from a PIPE investment I helped secure and the board voted for in 2000. A new investor, Crown Capital, led by former Michael Milken right-hand man and

Drexel Burnham partner Peter Ackerman, infused $25 million as a private investment in public equities that provided preferred stock dividends with super voting rights.

In the deal Zelnick Media was proposing, Crown Capital was not going to hit their target return—they'd get a reasonably good return, underpinned by their 10 percent annual dividend, but not the 20 percent plus internal rate of return that private equity investors seek. They opposed it and formed a board faction—ultimately including my long-time business partner—to oust me. It was an untimely and unpleasant exit in 2005, and I didn't take it well.

My gut said, "Walk away, cash out as much stock as you can, negotiate a severance deal, and—in the bigger picture—count it a win."

My ego said, "F*** you."

I secured the severance deal and stayed on the board for a few months until the stock tanked when it was announced that we lost the Subway business. The private equity guys were telling me, "Resign from the board, sell a bunch of stock, drive the price down, and we'll try to do a takeover."

Bottom line is, I got adversarial with the company when I might have been better served to accept the reality of the situation, no matter how infuriating it was. I had a strong track record in taking a company public and running it effectively, with a stock that outperformed our peer indexes. The press release when I left the company was glowing and positioned my exit as a mutual decision that, after ten years as sole or co-CEO, it was time to pass the torch. I had plenty of headhunter calls for exciting new positions.

My gut had been right that I should depart amicably and move on, and now I was headed for years of a corporate control struggle and litigation that would end up with the company in bankruptcy and my equity getting wiped out. Instead of meticulously selling the stock and moving on to my next chapter, I got hung up on the injustice of it all. Stubborn, proud, and blind to the tea leaves.

During the protracted proxy fight—I sued them, they sued me—I worked part-time for an investment bank called Diamond Capital

Advisors. I was in and out of Delaware Chancery Court, granted control of EMAK with a victorious proxy fight win, and then the lower court ruling was overturned by the Delaware Supreme Court. I was out again. It was the toughest couple years of my life, leaving a severely diminished net worth as a very tangible scar.

In hindsight, or through the lens of the business school EMAK case study, I could have "forced them" and said, "Listen, you buy back 75 percent of my stock, and I will go quietly." I could have just banked the money and wiped my hands of the situation and moved forward. Being a bulldog and never taking no for an answer is not always the smart thing to do. I wasn't accepting and embracing the reality of the situation. I was fighting after the bell.

But I didn't lack the confidence needed to cofound a hedge fund called Artemis Capital Partners as my next act in 2006 (while simultaneously pursuing the litigation against EMAK and still working part-time at Diamond Capital). I even put $5 million of my own liquidity in it (which represented most of my remaining net worth, including retirement funds). With tailwinds coming out of the mid-2000s, the markets were favorable for this next play. We raised money and invested with a strategy designed to be low-risk.

As the subprime mortgage crisis emerged in 2007, we felt poised to weather the storm. My old friends at Bear Stearns were the first bank casualty, collapsing in March 2008, its remnants rescued by JP Morgan Chase for a tiny fraction of what it was once worth. Old stalwart Lehman Brothers followed in September, with no bailout this time.

The unfathomable was happening.

The Dow Jones Industrial Average lost 4.5 percent, the largest one-day dip since the 9/11 attacks. The Federal Reserve jumped into action with emergency measures as panic mounted. Our fund of funds investment strategy was designed to minimize risk through extreme diversification of assets that historically were not correlated. We then used a complex, structured credit facility from BNP Paribas to put 3X leverage on this low-risk portfolio to juice the returns. We were holding on.

If we didn't expect the banking crisis, we certainly weren't prepared for the next body blow. Portfolios were taking a big hit, previously uncorrelated assets were all moving in the same direction—lower—and nervousness was ripe. Lots of big money was over-leveraged. People withdrew funds, bought gold, and stuffed cash under the mattress.

In December, news broke of the Bernie Madoff Ponzi scheme scandal. It was our death knell. My partner, who was our fund's chief investment officer, had always been skeptical of Madoff's remarkably consistent returns over every market cycle and assured me his due diligence screened for any Madoff exposure. He was wrong; a number of our underlying funds were invested in Madoff-managed assets. Because of our leverage, every loss got compounded three times.

It was a disaster. The bank called in their loans, and I had to close the fund and spend a year unwinding all the assets—paying BNP back in full—and returning all I could to investors. I took a $4 million personal hit. Ouch. Talk about a bad couple of financial and emotional years.

Good times, those aughts. I had a company go bankrupt, blew up most of my liquidity, had a lifestyle befitting a wealthy public company CEO, and no income. Not a productive formula for creating wealth! How does a proven capable guy with bona fide experience go from very well-off with a good deal of liquidity to in danger of living the rest of his life like a *schnook?!* I was sure hoping James Joyce's words would prove prescient, *"A man of genius makes no mistakes. His errors are volitional and are the portals of discovery."*[4]

It would be a disservice to hyperbole to say I underappreciated the risk of putting all that money into the hedge fund, which, by definition, implied an understanding of the term *hedge*. I should have moved on from EMAK, engaged in helping the company rather than actively hindering it. Our Beverly Hills lifestyle could have been significantly toned down. I wish I had set up some passive residual income streams. Shoulda, coulda, woulda. Plenty of feathers got ruffled, egos bruised, and eggs broken.

* * *

Through a mutual friend in LA, I met some guys who had left the storied advertising agency Chiat/Day to form a creative agency named Omelet, and we hit it off. We shared war stories of agency life, and they asked me to help as a consultant. I was getting paid $5,000 per month helping them navigate strategy, but soon realized they didn't have any experience operating a company. They were creatives, terrifically talented, and a not-so-quick study in Adam Smith's theory on division of labor. I joined their board and soon became chair. When a liquidity crisis hit in the second half of 2011, I was asked to raise some money.

"Don, you gotta get us some money!"

"Guys, I raised money for you a year ago, but you failed due diligence by not hitting your numbers." (We had secured a non-binding letter of intent with a prominent private equity company that would have injected substantial capital into Omelet.)

"Okay, look. Nobody is gonna invest at this point in a small, money-losing service business, even if they're cute as an omelet. What I'll do is this. I'll put in $200,000, which is literally all I have left, but I'm going to take control of the operation and become CEO."

There were three active partners at the time, and for cost reasons, one had to be let go. The other two remained with the company for several years and ultimately moved on. Omelet has, through various ups and downs (including surviving through a pandemic), maintained a positive trajectory ever since, and is a highly regarded, independent, full-service creative agency. I remain Omelet's majority shareholder and operate as executive board chair.

*　*　*

Like everyone, I've gone through personal and professional challenges over the years. Some of those challenges have been serious setbacks, reminders of the reality that is life. But they have always brought with them a lesson. I've found that the key is to be teachable and willing to learn the lesson.

In the immediate aftermath, I often chided myself for not knowing better, for putting myself in situations I could have avoided. But looking back, I can see that even those setbacks gave me new insight, particularly about trusting my instincts. If I had trusted my gut at the time, yes, I would now have a nine-figure net worth. I didn't always have hard data or factual evidence to request clarity or walk away, so I went along or pressed forward. But I've since learned to pay attention to my feelings of unease, even when I can't parse them definitively. I didn't always want to accept the reality before me, so I put on rose-colored glasses and convinced myself otherwise about it. Now, I look directly in the face of reality—and take it for what it is.

To this day, I am adamantly against settling. I've chosen discipline and hard work over ease and comfort. I don't believe in shortchanging yourself in the pursuit of where you want to be in business and in life. But at some point, everyone gets hit by a blow—sometimes multiple blows in rapid succession. In order to bounce back and recover, you have to get up and keep moving—this time, equipped with new insight.

The old adage that says life's all about lessons rings true for me. It does for us all. But its related adage, "Live and learn," is perhaps the most important. I've learned to take this adage a step further. It's not just about intellectually learning the lessons. It's about truly accepting the reality of what has happened, why it happened, and then embracing what you need to do going forward on whatever path you have chosen. And this embrace should be joyful and filled with excitement as you embark on your next journey, armed with newfound wisdom and conviction—with absolutely no regrets.

CHAPTER FOUR

You Can Accept, Embrace, and Overcome Any Challenge

A LARGE PART OF UNDERSTANDING THE BEAUTY OF ACCEPTANCE in life is learning to let go of things you cannot change. A little Monday morning quarterbacking is natural—"What could I have done better?"—but you need to find the positives to take away and leave the rest behind. Accept, embrace, and overcome. These are the things I wish I'd learned earlier.

The proverb "All is fair in love and war" is attributed to John Lyly's 1578 novel, *Euphues.* You don't have to read the book to get the gist: Life is fair, except when it's not.

When you're the youngest of three boys as I was, you learn this cruel, hard fact early. Whether—and when—you accept it is another story. It's a critical coming-of-age moment: you've been learning to play by the rules, and suddenly, that all goes out the window.

For me, that moment came at age twelve, in Little League.

I was a good baseball player, but for some reason I never got to pitch, even though I repeatedly expressed my desire to and pitched well in practice. Then, one day in the middle of the season, the coach gave me a chance. And I pitched very well—I had a lot of strikeouts. But the other pitcher was *very* good; we didn't score a single run on the other team, and at some point, they were able to score. Just one run. That was all I gave up that day. But it was enough, and we lost one–nothing.

After I got home that day, I ran up to my room, despondent.

I still played regularly. I was the third baseman, and I made the All-Star team that year, so it's not like I ended up sitting on the bench. And I was among the best hitters, so I batted third for the top team in the league, Gouz Dairy. (I still remember the tag line: "Gouz Rhymes with Cows!") But the coach never let me pitch again, even though I'd pitched a really good game—I think I gave up only two or three hits. But the unspoken message was, *Okay, we gave you your shot—and we lost the game.* Never mind that the other team was really good and our team couldn't score any runs that day.

In those days, your parents didn't go to the coach and say, "My little Donny's not playing! You need to put him in." If life handed you a raw deal back then, that was that—you just had to suck it up and live with it. Nowadays, a kid in my position would have helicopter parents who would threaten to sue the coach and get him fired.

Now, it's not like I'd be pitching for the Yankees today if I'd gotten my big break in a Little League game at age twelve. But I knew it was unjust, and it really stuck with me that I had no recourse. I gave up *one run*. Normally, Little League game scores were eight runs or more—there's usually a fair number of runs because players at that level make a lot of errors.

It was demoralizing, because the coach never explained it to me. He never came to me and said, "You know what, Don, you're too valuable at third base." That would've been a load of baloney—it's not like they already had Sandy Koufax and

Gouz (rhymes with cows) Dairy little league team (front row, second from left)

Don Drysdale on the roster—but at least it would have shown some kind of respect. To be perfectly honest, my control wasn't great. It would have been better if he'd just sat me down and said, "Listen, you have a chance to be a great third or second baseman. You're not big. You don't throw that hard. I think you're just better off at third base. You did a great job. We'll use you in relief sometime if we need it."

Instead, the message was, *We don't need you. You've been saying you want to pitch. Okay, you pitched—and we lost. Now shut up and go back to third base.* And that was it.

I don't know why that incident stays in my mind after all these years. Maybe you're thinking, *This guy is so sensitive; he's an emotional basket case who is not ready for the hard knocks of the real world.* I guess what it really comes down to is that there are events from everyone's childhood that still rankle. Those are defining moments.

I feel compelled to share this story because it felt so unfair. I had no recourse, and that's why it sticks with me. But, of course, life *itself* is unfair. Most people will suffer some form of injustice, however small, many times in their lives, and the only sane, useful response is to accept it and embrace the reality.

But what if there's more at stake than the score of a game? What if you're in a fist fight? One day, when I was in the fourth grade, I got a chance to test that scenario.

We were out at recess, and it was cold, so I had a hat on. Suddenly, another kid came up from behind me, took my hat, and ran away. I probably shouldn't use his name, so I'll just call him John, for the sake of the story. John was an Italian kid who had a reputation for being tough—not because he *was* tough, but because his family was in the Mafia. (Or, at least, that's what everyone at school thought.)

Everyone started laughing, and when I went after him to get it back, he threw it to one of his greaser friends. I ended up chasing my hat around for a minute—and then I just tackled him. Again, I'm not a big guy, and I wasn't big then, but I was a good wrestler. I could tackle. That's the best way to fight somebody who can outpunch you.

So I went in tight, wrapped my arms around him, and executed a single-leg takedown. And then I started pummeling him. I was really pissed—after all, he was embarrassing me in front of the whole class.

He grunted. "Are we gonna fight, or are we gonna wrestle?"

The question caught me off-guard. Was I breaking some unwritten street fight rule? Was I being unfair? Ridiculous! I had every right to match my advantage versus his. "I *am* fighting!" I said.

"Let's box," he said. "You can't tackle me! It's not fair!" He was pissed.

I didn't care. It was obvious to me that he was just mad about losing. What do you mean I can't tackle you? I'll do whatever I want. It's a fight!

Then, of course, I got in trouble because the teacher saw the fight. It's like in the NFL: Who gets the penalty? The guy who retaliates, not the guy who starts it.

To the best of my recollection, I don't think they suspended me or anything, but I wasn't able to go to recess for a week or two. And they probably called my mother. I didn't care, though. I was just proud of having stuck up for myself. Besides, *he* was the one who messed with *me*. What should I have done? Negotiated with him?

It was unfair that I got in trouble for someone else's aggression . . . but then, I guess some people might say it was unfair that I didn't box him according to Hoyle, like a fancy, old-fashioned gentleman. Heck, if John's family was as mobbed-up as the rumor mill had it, maybe he would've pulled a gun on me if we'd been just a few years older. How fair would *that* have been?

But what does the concept of "fairness" really mean?

The first thing we learn in life is to be fair. Then we wise up to the presence of deception and treachery. Now we have a dilemma. Have you ever heard someone say, *I cheated death*? Did you report them to the cheater police? Of course not; that's the key to survival. In

Fourth grade "fighter" at Dutch Broadway Elementary School

the animal kingdom, camouflage allows prey to hide in plain sight. Wings give birds an unfair advantage. And sharks, the apex sea predator, rule the depths with an ability to smell a single drop of blood in ten billion drops of water.

Totally *not* fair.

My advantages in sports, from the earliest age, were speed and quickness. They were followed by a strong will to compete, to *want it* more than others. This didn't make me a cheater, but it was an edge that an opponent might deem unfair, a mental state cast of the same unfairness I had accepted and eventually overcome through roughhousing with my brothers. The same goes for the bigger, taller kids who use their size advantage. But when it comes to rules of engagement—the do's and don'ts of a game—we expect adherence.

So you come into the world learning about rules, only to realize at some point that they get bent and broken. Life isn't a level playing field. There are advantages and disadvantages. You integrate the notion that the field tilts, and you learn to apply balance. The need to win at what cost? Do you need to cheat at stickball during recess? Your friends clench their teeth, call you a cheater, and the recess lady puts you in time-out. *Okay, okay, I get it. I won't do it again. Crime doesn't pay. Lesson learned.*

You learn similar lessons on the lacrosse and football fields. If you cross-check your opponent, you may get assessed a one-minute penalty. Commit a holding infraction, and the official marches you back ten yards. But sometimes you get away with it. And the opponent yells, "No fair!" (or something not printable).

During my sophomore year, in 1975, there was an incident in the first quarter of a game against our bitter rivals, the University of Maryland Terrapins (shortened to "Terps" by their fans or, as our team called them, "Twerps"). Until that game, we were undefeated for the season and were the defending national champions. Some newspapers called us the best team of all time. We were heavy favorites . . . and then we went down to College Park, where Maryland had already lost two games, and we got the crap beat out of us, 19–11.

During the first quarter, before the score became lopsided, I got tripped—a clear foul, but there was no whistle. I lost the ball, and my opponent scooped it up and passed it to an attackman, who scored a goal. The entire team came out flat that day, like a tire with the air let out of it. And that play seemed to illustrate that this was not going to be the Johns Hopkins Blue Jays' day. It was bizarre, as if we were drugged. We were so good, so overconfident . . . and then we went so flat, and they beat the daylights out of us. By the end of the first half, we were losing by a very large margin, and the game was essentially over—and remember, we were the best team of all time, allegedly.

Now, I'm not saying that incident started the avalanche. We might've already been down several goals; I don't remember. But it doesn't matter. It wasn't like we lost the game because of it. We weren't going to win that game. They were pumped, and we were flat.

Of course, I argued the no-call. But what can you do? The horn sounds, game over, and you live with the outcome. Emphasis on *game*. It's a war in metaphor only. Nobody's life is at stake. You get over it. That's how you learn. You can't argue with it. You just have to remember what the coaches always say: "Next play, next game."

But it was still dispiriting, because Maryland was our archrival. We were supposed to beat the hell out of 'em! And then, of course, after that shellacking we had PTSD; as the number-one tournament seed, we lost to Washington and Lee four days later, and we were finished. In four days, we went from being the best team ever to being knocked out of the playoffs in the first round.

The reason these stories are poignant to me is that they depict unfairness—something I have a hard time accepting. The unfairness of these incidents really stuck with me, and years later that sense of injustice underpinned my litigation with EMAK, as well as my conflict with that family friend who introduced me to the investment bank Josephthal. I had to prove that I would not be a *schmuck*. I would not be taken advantage of.

But those battles turned out to be more trouble than they were worth. In life, you will inevitably get stuck with unfair outcomes from time to time, and the injustice may linger. But if you don't let go of it, you are opening yourself up to far more problems.

* * *

What does it mean, all is fair in *love*? There's some irony hiding in there.

When you find love, you do whatever it takes to have it fulfilled. Often at great cost. This harkens back to the previous chapter about pursuing your passion until the flame goes out. Sometimes, this means lighting a new flame. It doesn't feel fair to the old one, but ultimately it is the best outcome for everyone. Where there's not a will, there's not a way, remember?

I've been on both sides of this. Stealing love, and having mine stolen. It's heartbreaking, yet it happens all the time. Whose fault was it that my first marriage ended in a painful and expensive divorce? Surely my ex-wife and I interpret the "facts" of what happened differently. Either way, our love light dimmed. It's a body blow when love deceives you, and it'll make you do crazy things.

The first impulse you have when you've been wronged is to "make it right." You appeal to Lady Justice for the scales to balance. In the old days, this might have meant grabbing a woolly mammoth tusk and going to look for the guy. Or, in a Kurosawa film, challenging your rival to a sword fight. Nowadays, you search out the best attorney—a term derived from *tournament*, like a jousting competition in Renaissance times. You hire someone better qualified to get in the ring and *joust* on your behalf.

What's the alternative—even the score yourself? Escalate an already emotionally charged situation by resorting to physical confrontation and violence? I mean, *all is fair in love and war*, right?

Society has evolved to serve justice in court rather than out in the parking lot or the street in front of the saloon. It gets messy the old way, where you walk ten paces, turn around, and may the best shot win. Instead of *dying for honor*, we now have, *Yes, Your Honor*. In the left corner, the plaintiff, and in the right, the defendant, each with representation to do their bidding in front of a judge and jury. It's a pretty amazing invention. Especially when it works!

There's a great scene in *The Man with the Golden Gun* where Francisco Scaramanga challenges his nemesis—and our hero—British Special Agent James Bond to an old-fashioned duel. May the best assassin win. At step nineteen (of twenty), Bond spins around and shoots, but Scaramanga has fled into a carnival set inside the cave. They *both* cheated! But wait, isn't that war?

Trust in justice is the bedrock of civilized society. Fairness, while a moving target, keeps the game from getting out of control. Sooner, not later, it is best to accept the balance of scales, even when it settles in someone else's favor. In sport and life.

In the previous chapter, I shared two injustices I faced. First, the family friend who surprised me with a large payment demand for making a capital introduction. Second, getting fired from EMAK. These experiences are the tip of the spear of unfairness I have become entangled with over my lifetime. While I was able to accept, say, an official's ruling on the lacrosse field, I was obsessed over not getting screwed in business. Whether it was a high-level proxy fight or an employee resigning right after a promotion so she could notch the higher title on her résumé, I wouldn't accept the grift.

My wife, Noelle, playfully calls it *Don Wants Justice*. I'm not the guy walking down the street who says, "Hold on—that guy looked at me funny; I need to go punch him in the face." But if you take advantage of my good nature and desire for fair play, and screw me, I will not let that stand. Some may say I have a problem (and they would be correct), but I have worked on it pretty effectively. That said, as my father would say, coining the old Yiddish phrase, "Don't get played as a schmuck."

This "justice will be served" mentality gets reinforced when you even the score on indignities big and small. I stood up for myself and my company during the IPO fundraising process because I firmly believed I was right. The court system through the appeal process affirmed this. Fairness won out—however, the cost was the relationship.

*   *   *

Ten years later, facing the indignity of being ousted as CEO of EMAK, I saw the scales of justice tilting away from me. I wasn't about to go without a fight. It was my view the company would benefit from going private, but a majority of the board of directors didn't agree. I ended up in years of litigation fighting what I firmly believed was an unjust outcome. It was a classic boardroom coup, with a controlling shareholder faction shifting the balance of power. Rather than accept the maneuver as a fait accompli—what's done is done—I pushed back, running my lance toward the imposing reality, tilting at this giant windmill with all of my resources.

I won some battles—enough to whet my appetite—but I lost the war when the company filed for bankruptcy. I was out millions, missing out on other opportunities, and for what, the dignity of justice? My personal justice, not the board's or the universe's. I couldn't accept being outplayed. I'd gambled and lost, and I wouldn't let go. It was a big mistake.

* * *

There is no medal of honor for the martyr who fights valiantly. No Don Quixote statue for the effort. *Here lies a principled guy who refused the short end of the stick. He threw pragmatism to the wind for a greater cause. He had no money left, so this is his modest headstone made of cement.*

I'm unsure what part of the body governs folly—the groin? My gut said, *Is this really a good idea? I'm in my prime with valuable CEO public company experience and lucrative opportunities to pursue.* Another part of me said, *They perceive you as weak and are trying to take advantage of your easy-going nature. You gonna let them get away with that?* Not smart. I think the gut has a better algorithm as a guide.

At some point, you have to use more finesse.

Have you ever tried to fix or assemble something while the person next to you said, "Don't force it—you'll break it."? You struggle to fit the square peg into the round hole, not realizing its futility. It's better to take a step back, read the directions, or consult a tutorial video online.

Or how about when you jump into bed with an early wakeup call— you've got a big presentation tomorrow—and you can't get to sleep? Your mind is racing, and you can't turn it off. The more you *will* it, the farther off the possibility of slumber seems. You're tempted to take a pill—anything to get you through the challenge of conking out.

A phrase I used before is, "You can't fight the tape." When the market starts trending in the opposite direction, fighting it won't help. Rather than double down on your bets, you should accept the loss. Own it. In other words, gently lay the hammer down. Try some hot herbal tea with honey and count sheep. Finesse beats brute force more often than not.

When a business school colleague of mine I hadn't seen in a while invited me out for a drink, he laid all this hardship on me: "I can't stand investment banking. I'm sick of the rat race. I only got into it for the money and because my old man pressured me in that direction. My marriage is a mess."

I listened and watched the poor guy order double scotches, one after another. He was a total wreck in a custom-tailored suit. He'd gone down this path and hit all the marks—career, money, fabulous wife with expensive taste, kids in private school, and a place in the Hamptons. But he was miserable.

By all appearances, this guy had the tiger by the tail. He was forcing the square peg into the round hole with a hammer, but how long could it hold? In my estimation, he was headed for a widow-maker coronary or a cocaine overdose. All I could say is, "Ain't it a shame."

How can this help you? When you face injustice or an obstacle, do you trust your gut to tell you which action to take? Do you fight to the death or do you take the medicine and live to fight another day? There's a lot of middle area there. There's no clear line in the shag carpet separating the two. Is it clear or opaque? Only your gut knows. The cost might be a substantial pay cut or a lawyer's fee to lay out the cost and benefits (at $1,000 an hour).

I got so good at listening to expensive legal advice, I felt like an expert. Attorneys marveled at how well I could read a brief. I ran out of red ink, marking up all the damn documents. *Hey, Google, do I need a law degree to take the bar exam?* I was only half-joking about practicing law. Running a publicly traded company and being in extensive litigation breeds ideas like this. Not only could I represent myself and save on legal fees, but maybe I'd also hang a shingle and charge others. I mean, why am I paying $500 to $1,000 an hour or more for this?

Let me share a joke: A corporate lawyer has a beautiful downtown penthouse. In his beautiful penthouse kitchen, the sink springs a bad leak. He calls a plumber to come and fix it. The guy shows up, patches the rupture, and hands him a bill for the work. The white-shoe attorney looks at it.

"This is insane—$825 an hour? I'm a corporate lawyer, and I only charge $750 an hour!"

The plumber just strokes his chin and says, "Yeah, that's what I charged when I was a corporate lawyer."

Equally funny is the notion that justice is fair. Consider that if you can't afford a defense lawyer, the court will assign you one at taxpayers' cost. If you *can* afford one—at $500–1,000 an hour—does that mean you're getting better legal advice? In our society, you often get the level of justice you can afford. This means the more emotionally and financially screwed you think you got, the higher the price you're willing to pay to balance the scale. And what are you guaranteed—justice? Nope, *bupkis*. The lesson here: *Unless you surrender the myth that life is fair, you are going to pay a very high price.*

We've all heard, and likely used, the phrase, "Don't take it personally, it's just business." As kids, we saw it in *A Christmas Carol* when Ebenezer Scrooge negotiates his share price for corn. The traders protest, "It's not fair!"

"No, but it's business!"

Fearing Scrooge's threat of tightening the screw even more and needing the deal, the buyers accept his terms.

And then, we see it again (with parental guidance) in *The Godfather*, in a scene featuring Sonny and Michael Corleone and consigliere Tom Hagen.

"It's not personal, Sonny. It's strictly business."

This exchange references a plan to whack a rival crime boss. Both instances provide the speaker the convenience of separating personal morality from that which is allowed to govern business. Society has advanced to the highly evolved state of humanity where all is fair in love and war *and business*. Accept the outcome, embrace the uncertainty, move on to the next deal.

* * *

I've always prided myself on keeping some sanctity in personal affairs. I don't think of friendship and romance as transactional. Everyday relationships aren't reciprocated in the same way—tit for tat. When you take the long view, it resembles more of the *do unto others as you want them to do to you* kind of exchange we learned. A return to the innocent bliss, that idealism of early childhood.

When I make a connection for somebody—a warm introduction, say—I don't expect an immediate return. I don't even tally it in some sort of karma ledger. I pass it forward. There is no scorekeeping. I know in my heart that when I help others, I am accruing a collective goodwill. A "thank you" is nice, but it is not always given. At least out loud. It might be implied or inferred through some nonverbal communication. Or not at all.

It's good to be at peace with that.

Even when things are clearly unfair in personal dealings, I find it easier to accept this unfairness. If somebody thinks I'm a jerk, I can live with that. It likely has more to do with them than me. I might try to find common ground, electing to make some small compromises to improve relations. I certainly won't declare war and spend emotional time worrying about getting even. *What, you don't like me? Fine—I'll sue you.* No. When people are petty and dealing with their own baggage, you show some grace and take the higher ground.

The Venn diagram where personal and business overlap isn't scientific. For most of my life, I acted as if it were. Somehow, I could take the high road and trust my gut about managing personal unfairness, and these instincts taught me how to take a body blow, choose my battles, and live to fight another fight (or love another love). Like when I accepted the fact that my debilitating knee injuries would hinder my lacrosse career. Then again, when I hung up my dancing shoes and embraced my graduate school studies.

In business, I always came out swinging, inclined to fight beyond the bell. Only recently have I seen that Venn diagram expand. I can be a man of character—not to be taken advantage of—*and* be virtuous at the same time.

I used to firmly say, "I don't negotiate with terrorists." That's nice, but sometimes you need your hostage back. Negotiation could be the best play when the other side believes as strongly in their convictions as you. Unless you want to keep paying the costs.

By the time I started playing lacrosse, I had learned to accept the occasional injustice as part of the game. Accept the call, embrace the outcome, and get ready for the next play or opponent!

The same goes for love.

In business, I reverted to a Pollyanna-ish mindset that fairness must be defended at all costs. Look where that got me! I can laugh about it because I now have the mindset to look at the positives. I can't change past outcomes, but I'm all the wiser for having gone through them. Call it lifelong learning. I'm more able now to overcome any obstacle or challenge.

I had a mentor who used to say, "Let's find the guy who said life is going to be easy and take him in the alley and beat the crap out of him." Life is not easy, and it is not fair. Yet we're encouraged to believe it is before understanding it isn't. Grasping this too early might make a kid cynical. Do we want three-year-old pessimists toddling around? As we mature, we don't have to get cynical, but we do need to become realistic. Realism means accepting. Accepting enables embracing the new and exciting opportunities that lie ahead, and that's a beautiful thing.

CHAPTER FIVE

Be Kind, Take Initiative and Work Hard, and Trust That Things Will Work Out

LATELY I'VE BEEN READING THE CLASSIC BEST-SELLING BOOK *Winning Through Intimidation* by Robert Ringer. Despite its title, it's not a how-to manual for bullying your colleagues, customers, and vendors into giving you what you want. Rather, it's an exploration of how some of us allow ourselves to be intimidated by daunting circumstances or by the forceful personalities of others, and it offers psychological strategies for standing firm in the face of such obstacles. The title reflects the author's belief that in any financial transaction, the person who is intimidated the most will earn the least.[5]

It's an enjoyable book, filled with good advice based on keen observations of human nature . . . but some parts of the book strike me as unnecessarily cynical.

First, in my opinion, Ringer undervalues the simple virtues of determination, discipline, and hard work. "If you keep your nose to the grindstone and work long, hard hours," he says, "you're guaranteed to get one thing in return: old! Hard work will not, in and of itself, ensure success." I think that's largely wrong, but let's put it aside for now, as I'll have more to say about this topic in the next chapter.

My strongest objection to Ringer's thesis is its presumption that most of the people you'll deal with in your professional life are out to get you, or are, at least, indifferent to the welfare of others. Seeing the world—especially the business world—as a vicious jungle, Ringer devotes three entire chapters to the idea that there are just three types of people in the world, and all of them are out to get you: "Type Number One" tells you upfront that he aims to take from you everything that you have; "Type Number Two" assures you of his good intentions before stabbing you in the back and taking everything you've got, and "Type Number Three" screws you and then is "sincerely sorry" afterward . . . but the result is the same, as if he weren't sorry.

I don't think that attitude is a healthy way to approach business, nor is it a healthy attitude to carry through life. I believe that a better way to live is to be kind, take initiative, work hard, and trust that things will work out in the long term. This isn't just a naïve, happy philosophy. My experience says it is the formula for success in business and in life.

It's all about maintaining an awareness of our common humanity. If you think the only way you can get ahead is by beating the other guy by any means necessary, you're not going to be kind. And if you think life is just going to hand you stuff and you don't have to work hard for it, then you don't take initiative and you won't ultimately get what you want.

But if you're kind, if you're human, if you're proactive, and if you have faith in people, then you know what? It's all going to work out, and everything is going to be okay. It may be readily apparent or it may take years before you realize how things all worked out, but things will work out for the best and you will come out ahead.

BE KIND

Meanness—or toughness, at least—has its place. But toughness will only get you so far.

Ringer is correct that it's no good to allow ourselves to be intimidated by aggressive behavior. The US Marines—at least as boot camp is portrayed in the movies—don't subscribe to my kindness-oriented world-view. Maybe they *can't* subscribe to it. It's necessary in that world to get everybody on the same page and thinking the same way in order to break down their individuality and turn raw recruits into disciplined marines.

But we're not doing that in the business world. We're not creating a fighting force. We don't want to destroy your uniqueness—we're *hiring* you for it! The last thing you want in the business world is a cookie-cutter employee. You want somebody who's creative, not somebody who's pro-grammed by abuse to shout, "Sir, yessir!" on command.

Well, an employee in the business world can't be creative if they hate their boss. They can't be creative if they're bitter at the company. They can't be creative if they feel their competitors are always out to screw them.

If you must criticize a subordinate employee, by all means be honest, even blunt. But don't be nasty or cruel—there's no point in it, because people don't *hear* cruel things. Rather than taking what may be well-deserved criticism to heart and resolving to do better, they start to get defensive. Then they start to blame you for the conflict because you're mean. Therefore, don't be cruel: there's no need for it, and it's usually counterproductive.

My father always said, "It takes more energy to be mean than it does to be kind." And that meanness energy is direct and strong . . . but it also makes you grind your teeth with bitterness and resentment. That's a diffi-cult way to live, and it creates a kind of negative doom loop. It also often ends in an early grave.

Instead, try just being kind to people. Everyone, more or less, is a good person. And even those who seem to be bad people . . . they suffer, too. You don't know what someone else is going through. Employing this phi-losophy because you truly believe it is a much more pleasant way to live. You will have closer friends, you will sleep better, and likely live a longer, healthier life. I believe you will also accumulate more wealth.

You have a business to run, so you're going to make whatever decisions you have to make, but there's no reason to be a jerk. There's no reason to be mean, unless you've caught somebody with their hand in the cookie jar, or blatantly defying your company values. Forcefully dealing with people who have clearly crossed the line isn't mean; it is protecting the integrity of your organization and its people.

*   *   *

So kindness is good. Everyone knows that . . . but what, exactly, does it mean to be kind?

Most of us would probably say that being kind means giving things to people, or doing things for them, or saying nice things to buoy their spirits. But there's more to it than that, and not everything we do that feels like kindness is actually kind to the people we're ostensibly trying to help.

I have a fairly broad definition of *kind*: Kindness is being both honest and respectful. Kindness is telling the truth, but not doing so in a cruel manner.

Now, sometimes that truthful approach might not come across as kind: "Tom, this is not the right business for you. You're not succeeding here, and we're both better off moving on. You're not going to get promoted here, and as soon as there's a business downturn, you're going to be the first to go. You're bright. You're nice. You're conscientious. You're far better off embarking on a career path that's going to be a better fit, or at least working for a company that's going to be a better fit. I will do my best to help you land in the right spot and provide enough financial runway so it isn't disruptive for you."

To me, *that's* being kind—although the person invariably doesn't take it well. They directly or indirectly blame you as the person making the decision. They're often bitter and don't leave on the best terms. This always bothers me, but it shouldn't.

Kindness can't mean hiding the truth or shading the truth. That's a hard pill to swallow, because it's not pleasant to tell somebody they're not making it. It's hurtful, particularly if they're a nice person who works their butt off. But some people just don't *get* your business. They just can't cut it, or they don't have the necessary work ethic, or whatever. And if you're a kind person by nature, it's tempting to let them stick around: "Oh, let's give them another month." I struggle with this dynamic to this day.

So why not do that? Because what happens next is the other people on their team start having to do more of their work. Soon they get tired of covering for the weak link in the chain, and they get resentful. They also start losing respect for you as a leader. So it doesn't ever end well when you keep someone around who is out of their depth. And at a company the size of Omelet, there's no place to hide. You're either really good, or you won't cut it. There's no learning curve that you're allowed unless you are a direct hire from college. We're too small, and we're competing in the top echelon of the creative world; we can't employ anyone other than very high performers.

It's a tough day at the office, having to let go of someone like that. But I have seen what happens if you don't have that hard conversation: Tom—he's nice, people like him, and he's trying his best, and you let him stick around for six or nine months. Then the business turns down, and now you *have* to let him go. And because money has gotten tight, now you can't give him much of a severance package. So you end up letting him go more abruptly than you would have—which is harder on him financially.

Or maybe he leaves on his own in six or nine months, because, deep down, people know when they're not making it. And often, because they know they're not making it, they leave—and then they're bitter, even though you didn't fire them. They knew they weren't getting promoted, they saw their peers get promoted ahead of them, and they became jealous, and somehow it's *your* fault.

What did it cost me to carry Tom for those six months? Let's see . . . he made $100,000 a year, so that's an extra $50,000 plus benefits I spent and got little in return for. There was also an opportunity cost of not replacing him quickly with a high performer. While I carried him, he spent half that time looking for a job. He never said "Thank you," and then, after he left, he bad-mouthed the company on one of those anonymous job boards. Morale at the company declined and it is a damn shame and unfair.

Compare that scenario with what would have happened if I'd just been honest with him from the get-go.

*   *   *

True kindness is being honest and empathetic, not just giving somebody a box of chocolates and being nice to them all the time. Being truly kind doesn't mean you're not decisive, and it doesn't mean you're not making hard decisions. But it does mean that nobody can question your motives. You're being upfront, and if people don't like it, well, at least you can go to sleep at night knowing you did the best you could do. You will also earn the admiration and respect of your colleagues.

That's what I mean by being kind. Kindness is empathy. It's not about fudging the truth so that somebody's feelings are not going to get hurt. When you try to do that, it's *un*kind. You're not doing anybody a favor by keeping them on, because the sooner they know that this place isn't for them, the sooner they can start looking for the next job that will be more fulfilling for them.

And if they're the right person, who embodies the company's values, you keep them employed while they do that. Obviously, you can't let them do that for six months . . . but for a month or two, you can help them transition into something that's a better fit: "I know you've got an interview, and we're both glad you don't have to hide it from me. Go. Don't worry about attending this afternoon's meeting."

Often, those people thank you afterward. They end up in a different industry, or maybe just at a different company where they're a better fit. Sometimes they even become a client.

*   *   *

You've probably heard the expression, "Hire slowly. Fire quickly." It's good advice. It's also really hard to do. Given the looming threat of lawsuits from disgruntled former employees, it's more important than ever today not to hire the wrong people, only to realize later that you've made a mistake, and then have to fire them.

But everyone errs from time to time, and when you've made a mistake, you need to acknowledge it. Be very careful about whom you hire in the first place, but if you find you've made a bad hire, face up to the situation and deal with it—because it hurts your credibility as a leader when you don't take care of a mistake.

Nobody will *tell* you that your credibility has been damaged, because you're the boss. But if you listen, you can almost hear your team members thinking, *Geez, if Don's keeping this loser around, then why am I busting my ass for him?* If morale is bad enough, you may even overhear stupid jokes: "She must have compromising pictures of him," or something similar. I've heard people whisper things like that over the years.

And even if they don't descend into conspiratorial paranoia, they'll still be thinking, *Why is this person still here?* It hurts your credibility, which is problematic—and that's why I can sleep at night after letting people go when I know they're just not making it. I'm not doing them any favors by keeping them around. Kindness has to come from empathy, but you cannot let empathy deter you from doing the right thing, even if the right thing is also the hard thing.

People say it's lonely at the top. It is. And if your goal is to be liked by everyone, you just can't win, because somebody will always think you didn't promote them when they should have gotten promoted, or they didn't deserve to get fired, or you made some other decision they didn't agree with. It's one thing after another. Therefore, your true north is, "I'm going to do the right thing, and I'm going to treat people fairly and kindly, and the chips will fall where they may." This is the only way to find peace as a leader.

It took me decades to learn to not obsess over whether I was liked by everyone. It matters more to me now to know I did the right thing, even if they don't know that or appreciate it.

In his book, *The Four Agreements*,[6] Dr. Miguel Angel Ruiz advises us not to take anything personally. Everything that other people say is a projection of their own subjective reality, not a result of something you did. When you are immune to the opinions and actions of others, Ruiz says, you won't suffer needlessly. You can't win if you're constantly seeking approval, particularly as a boss and a leader. Nobody ever thanks you for being "nice," particularly if they think you're wealthy, so you might as well just do the right thing, and whether they understand it or not is something you can't control.

*   *   *

Above all, then, kindness means being honest and respectful—and that applies to people outside your organization as well. Don't "ghost" people when they submit inquiries about doing business with you or about employment opportunities. If I interview someone or the company interviews someone and the applicant doesn't get any feedback, that is unacceptable to me. You need to close the loop and show that basic respect. You don't have to say, "Listen, you're the worst candidate I've ever seen." You just say, "We went with another candidate." You don't have to be mean, but you also can't leave them holding out hope by saying, "Oh, we're still making a decision," if you've already made your decision and they're out. You just tell them. It's common courtesy, and it doesn't take a lot of time. Remember that this is a human being. You're going to give them bad news, but you don't need to do it cruelly. You're doing them a big favor by being honest—in a kind way.

TAKE INITIATIVE AND WORK HARD

I'm frequently shocked at how passive many people are in the business world. Some of them seem to believe that God has such a detailed plan that your destiny is already written on a piece of paper in heaven, or that the universe works in mysterious ways and you just have to trust that whatever happens is *destined* to happen—and that this is an excuse for not taking initiative.

In my experience, it doesn't work that way. You've got to do everything in your power to put yourself in a position to be successful—and *only then*, after you've done that, you need to trust that things will work out however they're supposed to.

"However they're supposed to" includes the possibility that you will fail. But unless you do your part by being as prepared and staying as firmly in the game as possible to make sure you're in a position to succeed, that attitude doesn't work. It's not some kind of Zen, as some people seem to think; it's just fatalism. I don't believe the deal with God is like that. God doesn't let you sit around and watch Netflix and eat bonbons and then, somehow, you're going to get rich and the world's going to beat a path to you. If you sit around and eat bonbons, you're going to be a failure . . . and you *should* be. And God knows that you should be.

This outlook affects both your career and your relationships. You want to meet somebody and get married? Again, you can't just sit around and eat bonbons and watch Netflix. You need to look good—as good as you can look. You need to be successful. You need to go to parties where the right kinds of people are. You need to be your best . . . and then, if for some reason nothing happens, maybe that is your fate after all. (I have no familiarity with online dating, but ultimately I imagine the principles I am espousing hold true there, too. Fooling someone with an exaggerated online profile to get a first date almost assuredly will not end well.)

Regardless of what you believe God's role is in determining your fate, you've got to do your part. Don't expect anything for free, and don't imagine that because you're religious, it doesn't matter. Don't be one of those people who thinks their fate is already determined. Your actions directly influence your fate.

But if you do your part, then you just have to trust that it's enough. If it doesn't work out, *then* you get to back off, pivot, and say, "That's just what's meant to be. There is a different and better path for me ahead because this situation didn't work out." Your goals can't be allowed to go unaccomplished because you didn't show up and do everything you could do.

Now, the need to be proactive doesn't mean you should single-mindedly pursue lost causes. It's a cliché that you can't make an omelet without breaking a few eggs—but you also can't make an omelet if you open the carton and find that all the eggs are *already* broken. When the eggs are broken, know when to pivot. That doesn't mean quit and go eat bonbons; it means pivot to something else, using the knowledge you have acquired from the recent "setback."

In a sense, we're coming back around to the idea of truth-telling as kindness. There's a point where you have to say, "This ain't working." To be honest with yourself when what you've been doing isn't working . . . that's a kindness you do *for yourself.* Just as I'm not doing "Mary" any favors by keeping her on in a job she isn't good at and prolonging a career that's probably not the right path for her, I'm not doing myself any favors by sticking with a plan that isn't delivering the results I need. Same for a relationship. Be honest with yourself if it isn't going anywhere—acknowledge that "she just isn't into you."

* * *

In the interest of honesty, I should tell you . . . I myself have sometimes failed to heed the advice I'm giving you here. In my senior year at Hopkins, once I started getting into dance, I didn't train nearly as hard in the preseason on the lacrosse team. Given my two serious knee injuries, I needed to train harder than any of my teammates to be ready for the intensity of playing at the highest levels in the sport. My passion for the game was waning, and when practice started that January of 1977—by which time I was working at least three hours a night, six days a week for Arthur Murray—my heart wasn't in it like it had previously been. For the first time in my life, I was at risk of not being a starter, and of sitting on the bench. I deserved that, because I don't think I showed up with the best me I could have brought. Again, given my knee injuries, I needed to work twice as hard as I had before in order to make a full recovery, but I didn't.

But that's sometimes how we have to learn life's necessary lessons. Once you take the initiative *with the necessary commitment*, and as long as you're a kind and good person, things are going to work out. That should be enormously comforting.

TRUST THAT THINGS WILL WORK OUT

Taking the initiative is no guarantee of success—it's necessary, but not always sufficient. Again, you can't will an erection. If you've truly done what you can do to achieve an objective and the results you were hoping for haven't materialized, then for whatever reason, it's just not in the cards for you. You're not going to succeed in this. It happens to entrepreneurs all the time.

This is why it's important to know when to pivot—when to pull the plug. "We tried. We worked our butts off on this new product. We got it out into Walmart stores, and it didn't sell." And that thing you worked on, that you put your entire life savings and your family's money and your entire ego into . . . isn't going to sell.

I had a friend who started a great peanut butter enterprise, and Omelet did some work on the branding. It was all-natural, handmade peanut butter, almond butter, and cashew butter—and everyone who tasted it said it was unbelievable. They went to farmers markets, and everyone loved it. My friend, a super smart, highly successful entrepreneur, put a couple million bucks of his own money into it.

Now, at a high-end farmers market in Boca Raton, you can sell a jar of peanut butter for $15 or $20 . . . but you can't charge those kinds of prices at Ralphs, or even Whole Foods. And my friend's company could never get its supply chain to where it was feasible to charge less, and then they had distributors who took a large percentage, and then the retailers took a percentage, et cetera. So they could never sell enough to cover their costs. But they kept this struggling business going longer than they should have; they held on because it was their baby. They did everything they could to ensure success. They took initiative, they were nice, they were kind, they loved everyone . . . but it didn't work as a profit-making business. The broad market isn't willing to pay twenty dollars a jar for Fancy-Pants nut butters when you can get Jiffy for five. And they weren't prepared to compromise on the quality of ingredients and do all the other things they needed to do to cut their costs.

Despite its incredible efforts and the amazing quality of its products, that business was not destined to be successful at scale.

You may be wondering, *How do we get "trust that things will work out" from that story?* Well, when you've done everything you can, and things still don't work out, you just have to accept it. Whether it's God's will or just the way the world works, it's not going to happen for you, but things *will* work out, in some other way that you can't yet see or imagine.

It happens to entrepreneurs particularly often, because by nature, their hearts are always filled with optimism. We might hear that Whole Foods in Culver City had a 50 percent sales bump last week for our peanut butter . . . and then we realize that instead of only two jars, they sold three. But that's still a piece of data that says the trend is good, and so there must be hope.

But optimism is no virtue if it blinds you to reality. And it's easy to become unwilling to accept that reality because you've poured *everything* into that business. It's part of you. Entrepreneurs fail because they run out of cash, and they often run out of cash because they should have gotten the message earlier and pivoted to a different model. They fail because they are too stubborn or too blindly optimistic.

It happens in the stock market, too; people fall in love with a stock, and they won't sell it. They don't want to acknowledge defeat. They hold on while the price goes lower and lower, and there's a huge opportunity cost to doing that—to not moving on to your next thing.

It happens in romance all the time. You can't will a marriage partner if it's just not there. You look great. You took the initiative. You presented yourself well. You were nice to them. You tried everything. You even got work done—plastic surgery. Whatever can be done, you've done it all. But he's just not that into you. Why? Who knows. It doesn't make sense. You're exceptionally bright and successful. You're beautiful. You're sweet. But it just wasn't there for him, and you've got to cut your losses and move on. You did what you could, but the marketplace said this one was not for you. Move on. You have to take the universe's message. You need to pivot.

This is what behavioral psychologists mean when they talk about the *sunk-cost fallacy*. Whether in business, in romance, or any other realm of activity, it's a hard question: When do you cut the cord? When is the cost–benefit calculation not in your favor? When can you be sure that stock is just not going to move?

And maybe it *will* move in six months, but at this point, it's imprudent to keep holding on. *You've* got to move. You've got to absorb the lesson your failure has to teach you. An entrepreneur engages in constant haggling at this point: *Did we give this enough of a chance?* versus *I've got to cut my losses.* And sometimes, people will cut their losses too soon . . . but more often than not, you'll end up glad you pulled the plug and wishing you'd done so a little sooner.

"Trust that things will work out" doesn't necessarily mean they'll work out favorably for you. They'll work out how they're *supposed* to work out. And that's part of life. You need to look at the bigger picture. Everything doesn't always work out, and it's hard and it hurts for the first couple of weeks . . . but there is always a bright side. You've learned something from your failure. You've earned a PhD in reality. And in the longer run, the mosaic of life tends to work out for those who work hard, are kind, do their part, and listen to their gut and the marketplace as to when to pivot. Again, these puzzle pieces may take a decade to form, but they will, and you will look back with quiet contentment at how this unquantifiable algorithm of life works.

* * *

Whatever you're trying to achieve, it's going to work out the way it works out, but you won't have regrets if you were kind and took the initiative in the proper manner. And if it doesn't work out the way you wanted it to, there's a certain peace of mind to be had from knowing you did everything right, to the best of your ability. You've got no regrets, because you didn't screw people over and you didn't expect good things to happen without your putting in the work. If this is how you conduct yourself, you can rest assured that another, more prosperous door will open for you.

No, you did everything you could, and it just didn't work out the way you were hoping it would. Take some peace, learn the lesson, and move on.

CHAPTER SIX

Outworking Everyone Else Beats Being Smarter Than Everyone Else Every Time

THERE'S AN OLD SAYING ABOUT HOW LIFE CHANGES ONCE YOU finish school: the B students hire the A students, and the C students donate libraries.

Now, obviously that's a bit simplistic, but there's a nugget of truth at the core of it: intelligence is somewhat overrated as a predictor of success, because hard work trumps it every time. People think that being smart is a ticket to instant wealth. It is not.

At the risk of boasting, I'm willing to say that I'm a reasonably smart guy . . . but I am definitely not smarter than everyone else around me. I don't *have* to be smarter than everyone else, however, because there is a more reliable way to make up for smarts—and that's honest, hard work.

I wasn't born with this understanding; like most people, I came to it through hard experience.

In the last chapter, I emphasized the importance of being flexible enough to change course when it becomes clear that you're on the wrong path—of knowing when to pivot. There are pivot points in every person's life, defining moments when we have to realize we've reached a dead end and need to find a new direction. For me, one of those moments came when I realized it was time to walk away from lacrosse and get serious about dancing.

As I've said, another such moment came when I was at Columbia. My first semester grades were really bad, and my father made it a point to tell me he wouldn't pay for an education if I was going to continue partying instead of studying. I knew I didn't want to work at Arthur Murray for the rest of my life. (I mean really—degrees from Johns Hopkins and Columbia, and you go to work as a dance instructor?!) I realized that I needed to do something I was uniquely good at. I also needed to quit spending so much time meeting pretty girls and making glamorous friends, and instead, get very good in business unless I wanted to end up an also-ran without any money, which was a very, very scary thought. So I started studying more—a lot more.

The common thread connecting all these phases of my life—lacrosse, dancing, schoolwork, and business—has been hard work. I outworked people in sports, I outworked people to learn to dance, and I outworked people once I decided to study and then pursue my career. I would work hard at whatever I was into at the time. I didn't care if that meant eighty hours in a week, or a hundred hours. I had no threshold. I worked late into the evening, and I worked through weekends. It didn't matter.

*   *   *

Don't get me wrong; I'm not saying that natural gifts like intelligence and athleticism don't matter, or that they don't provide a strong advantage. In the athletic field, for example, when you get to the top, you can't just rely on outworking everyone. If it takes you five seconds or longer to run the forty-yard dash and you want to be a wide receiver, you are not going to play pro football; I don't care how hard you work. And there's an equivalent barrier in business: If your IQ is under one hundred, then no matter how hard you work, you are probably never going to be a CEO of a Fortune 500 company.

Therefore, it's not just about who works hardest; it's about who works the hardest *and gets results*. You could work hard and *not* get results, either because you're not smart enough or you don't listen to the marketplace and keep pursuing dead ends. Working hard is no ticket to anything—it's necessary, but not sufficient.

So yes, natural advantages do matter. But an advantage can be squandered if you don't have the grit to do the hard work of maximizing it. When I started working at Arthur Murray, I wasn't rehearsing the rhumba in front of a mirror ten hours a day. Dancing came to me pretty naturally, and frankly, I made up half of what I taught my students.

Lacrosse was another story. As I've said, I'm not a big guy, and being on the smaller side and trying to compete in contact sports was . . . well, let's just say it was sometimes humbling. If you're a big man, they take one look at you and say, "Oh, this guy is six-feet-two, 220 pounds, and reasonably fast, so we're going to find every way to get him on the field."

I think that was a driver for me. When you don't have an advantage like that, you just have to show that you're tougher and don't make mistakes. You do whatever you must do, because five-foot-eight guys don't *have* to be put on the field. So I just did what I seemed to *have* to do.

I loved the game, but loving the game isn't enough, especially if you don't have the physical gifts—height and weight—that would give you an advantage. So you have to work harder to compensate. I didn't love having to relentlessly train with weights, wind sprints, stick drills, et cetera, but I loved the end result.

And it was the same at Columbia, when I had to quit dancing and take my studies more seriously if I didn't want to be the oldest guy in the club still working at the deli. I had to outwork people. I was smart, but I wasn't smarter than most of the student body at Columbia. I couldn't just fall back on brilliance. I had to study a lot and work hard.

And that hard work paid off. I worked my way into a position as a research assistant for one of the school's top professors. I was elected president of the American Marketing Association, Columbia Chapter. I even became an adjunct assistant professor when I graduated, teaching an advanced marketing class to Columbia MBA students. I was smart enough to turn myself around, but I did it through hard work more than brilliance. I don't think I could have succeeded in athletics the way I did—or in business, or at Columbia—without that intense work ethic. I learned what the remarkable inventor James Dyson declared in his autobiography, *"We always want to create something new out of nothing, and without research, and without long hard hours of effort. But there is no such thing as a quantum leap. There is only dogged persistence—and in the end you make it look like a quantum leap."*[7]

Intelligence can probably get you to the top of your grammar school class, but as the pyramid gets narrower on your upward path to success, you have to compete with more smart people. To return to my football analogy, I would imagine that if you were to show up at Ohio State's spring football program as a freshman, having been a high school All-American, you'd look around and say, "Wow, there's a hundred people here, and they are *all* high school All-Americans. They are all as big as me, and they are all as fast as me!"

Then it becomes a matter of your work ethic. There's an early point where you can separate yourself from the masses by natural ability . . . but later there comes a point when you try to make it to the big time, and you find yourself in the company of a lot of competitors who have the same talents you have. And when you reach that point, outworking and out-hustling is your only option.

*   *   *

Even within the realm of what we loosely define as "intelligence," there are more valuable traits to have than raw cognitive ability. That kind of raw intelligence is essential in certain fields, obviously; if you are inventing a new drug or are building a new semiconductor chip, it is raw intelligence and know-how that make your work possible.

But in most contexts, *emotional* intelligence (sometimes referred to as "EQ") beats academic intelligence, as long as you have a threshold of capability. How do you deal with people? How do you read the room in order to sell? How do you know when to say something and when not to? As artificial intelligence becomes more and more prominent in the workplace, the importance of EQ as a differentiator will become even more important.

Even in sports, emotional intelligence is at least as important as raw intellect, and maybe more so. How to get along with teammates? How is the captain selected?

In many situations, EQ beats IQ. And unlike cognitive ability, emotional intelligence is, to some degree, within your control. You can develop your EQ by learning to become more self-aware, which in turn enables you to realize when your ego is taking over in a social situation. That understanding keeps you grounded in reality, which helps to prevent minor conflicts or disagreements from spiraling out of control.

* * *

Many people believe that most or all of their problems stem from something beyond their control—who your parents were, whether you had money growing up, what school you went to, et cetera, and that "it doesn't matter how hard I work, the chips are stacked against me. No matter what I do, I won't be able to make it because the other guy has had every advantage and it's just not fair."

That classic victim-type mentality is the antithesis of "I am going to outwork everyone." And it's incredibly unhealthy. Underlying it is the idea that the other guy doesn't deserve his success, and so his happiness constitutes some sort of injustice. He didn't earn it; he's just lucky.

To be sure, luck does play a role in success. Some people are born into wealth—and although many such people work hard to retroactively "earn" their good luck, many others don't. For the majority of us who weren't born into wealth and have had to work hard for our success—well, we, too, depend on at least getting a small lucky break now and then. There are also poor people who are fortunate enough to have a fantastic teacher who mentors them and shepherds them through childhood. That's lucky for them, even if the circumstances of their birth are not.

But you can't just be a resentful, willful victim. It is unhelpful. The truth is that life is not fair. There may well be reasons to say, "I didn't have as good a shot as somebody else." Maybe that's true. But so what? It is what it is. I'm not six-foot-three, so I could never play pro football. That's not fair, I guess.

Some people take the resentment train even further and develop a feeling that anyone who is more successful than they are must have come by their success dishonestly, or at least unfairly in some way. Many subscribe to the notion that "behind every great fortune is a crime." If you're doing well and I'm not, then you must have cheated.

I don't see that. Are certain people more ruthless and cutthroat? Absolutely. Are some of them underhanded? Absolutely. But I don't see cheating as a way to get ahead. The world is largely a meritocracy, and although some people are born smarter and some people have better connections or otherwise have a leg up, I really believe that if you work hard enough and get a little luck, you can achieve virtually anything within the range of your abilities. (At least if you live in the United States or another democracy.)

You have no say in what kinds of advantages you're born with—how smart you are, or how wealthy your parents are. You can't control how tall or how well coordinated you are. You can't control certain inherited predispositions toward weight gain or depression.

But you *can* control how hard you work, and that counts for a lot. And therefore you should do it. Do other people have natural advantages like smarts or money or nepotistic connections? Sure—because, again, life is not fair. You just have to accept that and move on, because the one thing you can control is your effort. As famed author and marketing guru Seth Godin said, "While luck may be more appealing than effort, you don't get to choose luck. Effort, on the other hand, is totally available, all the time."

You can control whether you go for a walk or exercise. You can control (to an extent) what you eat. You can control your work ethic through discipline and passion, and by focusing on your end goal. If your end goal is to be a starter on the team, if your end goal is to be reasonably successful, if your end goal is to graduate in the top 10 percent of your class, you can control a fair amount of what causes that to happen or not happen.

Irrespective of the barriers you may face, nobody can take these things away from you: your effort, your work ethic, how you treat other people—all are within your control.

So my message to you is this: never forget that you control your own destiny. It doesn't matter how you grew up. And stop looking for excuses. There are plenty of them out there, and some are legitimate . . . but so what? Stop looking for problems, because you'll always be able to find them, and you'll always be able to blame something.

People love to find problems that are outside themselves. They can point to those problems and suck their thumbs and feel better. It's a lot easier than looking at yourself in the mirror and saying, "You know what? I'm not good enough for that position," or "I didn't work hard enough," or "I made a really bad judgment call on that one." It's a lot easier to blame someone else—and it gets even easier if you have an entire support structure, whether it is your parents or your friends, who are all saying, "Poor Johnny, they only want Ivy League graduates for their professors or CEOs, and there's nothing you can do about it."

When the problem is outside of you, there's nothing you can do about it, and almost by definition that makes you a victim—which you may *want* to be, because then you don't have to be responsible for fixing anything. But if the problem is in you, then surely that's better, isn't it? Because then you can fix it.

And essentially *every* problem is within you. There is always a workaround. There is always a way forward if you are determined enough. It's not about just blindly marching forward; you have to be pragmatic. You have to work your butt off, be a good person, and take the initiative. Go out and find something you're uniquely good at, something there's a sizable market for, with no dominant competitor to prevent you from breaking in (this applies to finding the right job as well as being an entrepreneur).

Me teaching dancing in Baltimore is a perfect example. I was an above-average dancer in New York in 1976. New York was truly in its own world then, because that's where disco and everything really emerged. So you had a proliferation of dance studios like New York Hustle, and there were great dancers, far better than me. (If nothing else, they had been dancing for a long time.) But Baltimore was like an entirely different planet. It was a year or so before *Saturday Night Fever*, and the disco era hadn't really begun down there, so there was no such thing as Studio 54. That meant that in Baltimore, I was the coolest, best dancer on earth, so when I decided that I could teach dancing, I had a market all to myself. I had plenty of competition in New York; I had none in Baltimore. I was the one-eyed man in the land of the blind, and I capitalized on it right away. I could never have done that in New York.

* * *

I want to wrap this chapter up by talking about the benefit of having a role model—a boss, a teacher, a mentor, or anybody who holds you accountable and inspires you to work incredibly hard.

When I graduated from Columbia Business School, I went to JCPenney, where I was a superstar because they had very few MBAs, and my analytical skills stood out. I left after two years because my gut told me, "You do not want to stay at JCPenney, for the sake of your career." Even though I was doing really well, their pay scales were relatively low, and of course, that was the right decision in hindsight because they ended up going bankrupt. But even then, I knew they had no competitive advantage. Sears was bigger and better, and a company called Walmart was growing exponentially. So my gut told me to get out. Time to pivot.

When I left to go to Coopers and Lybrand's management consulting business, I had the kind of moment I described a few pages back: the pyramid had narrowed as I climbed it, and I was no longer competing with mediocrities. *Uh-oh*, I thought. *Everyone here is smart, and everyone has an MBA.*

My boss was a hard-nosed South African guy, and let me tell you, I would imagine 95 percent of people would have quit with this guy as their boss, because he was *tough*!

"Kurzy," he said, "nobody gives a damn what you think. You have no right to give your opinion. You're young, you have no experience, and these people are paying us to give them advice as a consulting firm. You have no right even to *have* an opinion. The only thing you can say is what you can prove." He taught me how to think in structure like that.

He was a bear about typos and other tiny details. (Back then, of course, there was no such thing as spell-check.) You'd work all weekend, and all night. You'd pore over everything, and he'd just point to a word that should have been capitalized or a typo or a misspelling.

And he would rip my analytical work to shreds, because I would have facts interspersed with conclusions and recommendations. He said, "No. In the Findings section, there is no opinion, and your conclusions are the same ones any moron would reach based on those findings and facts. Recommendations should fall out of the conclusions." He hammered that into me.

So he beat the crap out of me. I would literally do anything he said . . . and every Friday night, he would rip up my work and I would have to work the whole weekend. For a whole year.

And he made me very good.

It wasn't my pride, necessarily. I didn't say to myself, *All right, then, I will show him! F.k him!* I just said, *Okay, I'm not doing it right, so I need to keep redoing it.* And one day, I just *got* it. And then I was a star, receiving a promotion to supervisory consultant shortly thereafter. I even followed him to Cresap, McCormick and Paget (which ultimately morphed into Willis Towers Watson) when he left Coopers and Lybrand so I could continue to work for him.

It's not that working with him raised my IQ or my SAT score; it's not like working there made me smarter. It's just that by working harder, he taught *me* to work harder.

And I listened to his criticism. I had enough humility to think, *He must be right. He can't just be making me redo things because he's mean.* (Although I'm sure there are people like that.) And finally, it clicked. But if he hadn't hammered it into me like that, it might never have clicked.

That experience has served me well to this day. But I don't know if I could have benefitted from his peculiar style of mentorship (if you can even call it that) without the grit to be able to keep reworking my analyses, and saying, "How is *this*?" And then getting it ripped up again. And then coming back again and again. I don't think most people would do that. They would say, "To hell with him, I'm going to go back to JCPenney where they love everything I do!"

So I think my work ethic really paid off there, just as it did at Hopkins, enabling me to be a key midfielder as a freshman on their first NCAA national championship lacrosse team.

This is good news for anybody who thinks that success goes only to the connected, to the powerful, or to the children of the wealthy. Maybe to some extent it does, and you *can* be bitter and resentful toward those people.

But you will be miserable, and you'll be at the mercy of your emotions, and you'll drift aimlessly on the currents of life. That's no kind of life for me. I like being in control of my destiny.

And I accept reality. Some people allow their vanity to make them anxious about their age. I used to be like that, but not anymore. I work hard to look the best I can, and am very diligent about my diet, exercise regime, and sleep, but my age is my age, whatever it is. Others lose sleep fretting about how their lives should have been. Not me. I've made plenty of mistakes, and my net worth is a lot lower than it should be . . . but I take a lot of comfort in knowing that I can still do anything I want. I'm in control of my life, and no one can ever make me feel helpless. That is a beautiful feeling, and it is available to anyone.

CHAPTER SEVEN

Don't Get Trapped by Regrets

EVERYONE KNOWS REGRETS ARE POINTLESS. THAT'S WHY WE have idioms like, "Don't cry over spilled milk." The best coaches always say, "Forget about that fumble; just concentrate on the next play." Or if their team loses, it's, "Just focus on the next game."

It can be maddening, though. You lose a game on account of a bad ref call. You drop a pass that should have been a touchdown. The field goal kicker hits the upright. When things go wrong in certain particular ways, there's a feeling—nebulous and hard to put into words, but nonetheless powerful—that things somehow *should have* gone differently.

It can be really hard to move on from that feeling, but a feeling is all it really is. Those best coaches are right about "the next play," because the antidote to regret is constantly looking forward. Whatever mistake you made, you have to acknowledge it, and you have to learn from it. You can't just bury it and forget about it, because if you do that, it comes back—but neither can you obsess over it and bury yourself in recriminations. You have to face it, and you have to accept it and embrace the lesson it has to teach you.

It is helpful to believe that a negative event somehow will lead to good things going forward. And often it does, even if you can't see it at the time.

You just have to accept that it's God's plan, and that's your journey. You don't need to be happy about that setback; you just have to accept the reality and trust things will work out over time. That has been my experience.

When a negative event is not your fault—the ref made a bad call, or you made a mistake that thousands of other people made, like trusting Bernie Madoff with your money—it is a little easier to absorb (though the injustice of things like bad ref calls can leave you bitter if you let them). But when you've made a clear decision, even though your gut was telling you something different, and that decision turns out to be wrong, it's hard to accept, but it's incredibly important to do so.

* * *

Like anyone, I have my own experiences with regret. My first marriage ended in a very expensive divorce, and I lost a large amount of money fighting a war against my old company—a war that left nobody better off, and that I should have just walked away from.

When the time came to let go of my marriage, we negotiated a settlement agreement and avoided litigation—and over my lifetime, of all the things I've lain awake at night grinding my teeth about, that isn't even in the top five. The EMAK war, and the IPO fundraising incident . . . those things bothered me a lot. But the end of my marriage did not. I did a good job letting go of regret on that one. I accepted that I made the decision to get married and that the evolution of the marriage, which included some wonderful periods, was what it was, and that it was time to move on. Even absorbing the large payouts to my ex-wife was something I accepted, though it placed a significant financial burden on me. Relatives and friends over the years kept saying, "How can you pay all this money to your ex? It isn't fair, and what did she do to deserve that windfall? There weren't any kids!"

My response was, "I made the decision to marry her and I must live with the consequences." Yes, that was literally my response. And, quite significantly, I recently got remarried to my true soul mate Noelle, and that is an incredibly good outcome.

I know people who have divorced and never gotten over it. Their wife cheated on them, and then they just couldn't move on. They were too bitter. In one instance, the guy even got remarried, but it was his way of saying, "I'll show her!" His heart wasn't really in that second marriage, and he wasn't really head over heels in love with his new wife. He was acting out because he'd never let go of the hurt from his previous marriage, and it was a terrible thing to witness. He'd fallen in love with the perfect lady, and he felt like he could never get anyone as good as that again—and he was right. And then he couldn't stop talking about it, and it became unpleasant to be around him.

I get the disappointment, I get how hurtful it is. I get that you can see injustice in the situation. We all experience that. But there's a grieving point and then there is a healing point.

I've learned to accept and embrace my mistakes and failures. In retrospect, I made a mistake; rather than taking that introduction to Josephthal from that old family friend, I should have used a different underwriter. It would have saved me going to court and having all that negativity and bad blood. That kind of thing can linger in your heart for the rest of your life, if you let it.

Here's another mistake I made: I should have fully supported the new management team at EMAK when they fired me. I did negotiate a good severance package, and I should have just stayed on the board and worked out an agreement to sell them my stock. The consequences of fighting it rather than cashing out were terrible, but it was just a big mistake. It was time to move on, but I couldn't take that reality. It was ego-bruising that they fired me from my own company, but I wasn't exactly playing high-level chess. I had so much leverage at that time—I had the biggest client relationships—that I could have essentially forced them to buy my stock. But once I resigned from the board and initiated a proxy contest, that was all over.

But it was just a mistake, albeit a very large and expensive one. And even smart people make them. It is easy to drown in regret over a decision like that, because you knew in your gut you shouldn't have done those things. But your pride, your sense of justice, overtook you.

So how do you move on, versus wallowing in *I can't freaking believe I put myself in this untenable situation*? When the EMAK debacle was finished, I had pissed away what was once tens of millions of dollars. I knew that I could very well never make that type of money again. How did I sleep at night?

By keeping the underlying mistake in perspective: it was just a bad decision, underpinned by a very bruised ego. And everyone makes them. And if you don't truly accept and embrace that bad decision, you are destined to a life of misery and bitterness.

* * *

Some people survive their regrets, and some people get taken down by them. Sometimes a door shuts . . . and then a new one opens, because you move on and you accept and embrace the reality of what has happened. You see cancer patients who, after they get diagnosed, say, "Okay, I'm going to do everything I can to heal, and I'm going to change my diet, and do whatever I need to do, and then it's all in God's hands." And then they go into remission and their sense of purpose is rekindled.

And then there are those who say, "Woe is me and screw it, I never smoked, yet I got lung cancer. I only have a couple of years to live, and I'm going to spend them in bitterness." This attitude can ruin whatever time they have left and really hurt the people they love. That negativity and its physical manifestations can also minimize their chances of going into remission.

Most entrepreneurs have one, two, three, or even four failed ventures before they finally succeed. But they learn from those failures, and, in fact, investors sometimes *like* somebody who has had a failure. Why? Because they see that person as seasoned, as someone who has made enough mistakes to have learned a few things, and who won't repeat that mistake. From an investor's point of view, an entrepreneur who succeeds at his very first venture may have just gotten lucky, and could screw up this time and blow their investment.

Some people who get fired from a job are bitter at first, but then they end up in a different career that makes them happier, or with a company that is a better fit for them, and they end up much better off. That goes a long way toward enabling them to let go of their bitterness.

If you are suffering from regret, you don't open yourself up for what's next. You are still living in the past. And that is fundamentally against the accept-and-embrace ethos I've been advocating in this book.

I've lived out both of these scenarios—wallowing in regret versus accepting and embracing reality. And I think at this point, I've gotten quite good at the latter.

My current business presents endless opportunities for regret. Sometimes we lose a pitch we shouldn't have lost, and that's disappointing, of course. On the other hand, sometimes you can regret winning. That happened to us at Omelet recently. We won a very competitive, months-long pitch for a high-profile client. Between freelancers and our own staff, we spent probably a half a million dollars on this client . . . and they ended up not doing anything. They didn't pass on the pitch, they didn't move forward with the work—they didn't do *anything*! They just led us along. They kept saying, "Oh, can you do one more version? We are going to take it to our CEO now, so can you do *another* version? Tweak this idea, tweak that one . . ."

And then, in the end, it was all for nothing.

What did we do? We moved on to the next pitch. We did write a letter to them, saying how inappropriate this was, and how abusive it is to do this to an independent, self-funded agency like Omelet. They should have told us there was a chance that they were not going to do anything, and we said so in the letter. But then it was time to move on. You've got to get to the next one. This is a lousy business in some ways—clients will take free work and try not to pay you. We could have stewed over it for months, wishing we'd never done business with that client or insisting we wouldn't do any revisions unless we were properly paid, but I have learned to apply the accept-and-embrace ethos to situations like that, instead of living with regrets. And, of course, we will do everything humanly possible to never let that situation happen to us again.

I don't know whether there is some master plan governing our lives, but I've learned that it's better to accept that, for some reason, this kind of setback is part of your journey, and it will lead to better things. But you have to do your part, like working very hard, taking initiative, and acting ethically, and you have to be open to new opportunities as they present themselves.

I did better with the hedge fund; I acknowledged it was not going to work after the Madoff scandal and market blowup precipitated by the Lehman Brothers bankruptcy. My partner wanted to keep it going, but I realized this thing was never going to bounce back after all those losses, and I had to move on—so I immediately moved to close the fund, pay back the bank, and return as much money as possible to investors.

*   *   *

One source of regret is an emotional response to the world: anger and frustration. You become angry with yourself over something in your life that doesn't work out the way you think it *should have*, and that regret simmers in your consciousness and slowly ripens into a constant state of anger.

Do you remember *The Honeymooners*, one of television's earliest sitcoms? In one episode, Ralph Kramden, your favorite bus driver, sees a doctor in hopes of finding a way to manage his nervousness and anger. The doctor tells him, "Whenever you're all steamed up, just say this phrase: 'Pins and needles, needles and pins, it's a happy man that grins,' and then say to yourself, 'What am I mad about?'" Ralph goes home in a good mood, much to his wife's surprise.

Ultimately, however, it doesn't work. He soon gets into a conflict with his landlord and blows his top so badly that he and Alice get evicted. (A similar story unfolds on an episode of *Seinfeld* in which George's irascible father, Frank Costanza, tries to manage his own constant rage by shouting, "SERENITY NOW!")

It didn't work for Ralph, it didn't work for Frank, it doesn't work for me, and it won't work for you. Serenity, like an erection, cannot be willed.

I find that it's more effective to face the causes of your regrets and frustrations head-on, without trying to distract yourself or rationalize them away. Just accept the cold reality of the situation:

"Boy, that was a really messed-up thing that happened!"

"Damn, this marriage is irreparable at this point. There is a long, difficult path ahead that I need to prepare for."

"The ref clearly blew this call and the entire trajectory of the game turned from that point forward."

"Oh no, this company is not going to make it," or "Rats, we're not going to win this piece of business," or "What a damn shame, I'm going to have to fire this wonderful and loyal person."

Delaying and distracting does not work. It just creates ulcers. The problem doesn't go away. It's like taking aspirin when you have a bad cavity: it might work for a week or two, but it doesn't work in the long run, and that's how you get an abscess.

Meditation (which I'm not very good at) teaches this. Be in awareness, be in the moment. Meditation teachers will tell you that there is no good or bad emotion. It's not healthy to respond to a "bad" emotion by saying, "I just want to get rid of it. I want to go back to feeling good." Everything is awareness, and an emotional reaction is just one more thing to notice and be aware of: you observe it and you let it go, good or bad.

You can look at your life as a puzzle or a mosaic, or maybe as a graph: there is no such thing as a straight line to success. You have to be able to absorb your setbacks and learn from them. That doesn't mean you don't regret some things you've done—after all, there are people who spend five or ten years in prison and regret doing whatever put them there. But then, those with self-awareness come out with a new purpose and new energy to go and accomplish something.

I actually know a little something about this firsthand. I was executive producer on a 2015 award-winning documentary movie (produced and primarily funded by Omelet) called *License to Operate*.[8] The whole thing came about because I was on the board of a non-profit organization called A Better LA, which was co-founded by NFL coach Pete Carroll, when he was head coach at USC, during a period of major gang violence between the Bloods and the Crips in Los Angeles.

The purpose of the organization was to reduce gang violence in Los Angeles. Carroll saw that a lot of kids from Compton and East LA were great student athletes, and he started noticing that some of them would linger for a long time after practice. They didn't have a nice, safe place to go back to because they lived in such crime-ridden, gang-dominated neighborhoods, and they wouldn't really talk about it.

The idea of A Better LA was to recruit ex-gang members, many after they'd served their prison time. Some of these people were the worst of the worst, who now had a mission to go and heal the neighborhoods they'd once helped destroy.

The movie was called *License to Operate* because that kind of "license" was something only these ex-gangbangers could bring to the effort. You can't very well send a social worker in a bow tie into Compton to say, "Hey, you guys stop fighting. Okay? Be nice! Let's all just go and (checks slang dictionary) 'shoot some hoops!'"

People like that have no license to operate in those neighborhoods. They may get beaten up—or worse. But these ex–gang members have the credibility to walk those streets, to talk to people, and to be listened to. They have the *license* to go in there. And their goal was to stop the retaliatory killings that often caught "civilians" in the crossfire.

As soon as those fully trained mediators sponsored by A Better LA would hear of a homicide, they'd go right to the scene, working closely (but not *too* closely, in the public eye) with the LAPD,

Documentary film poster for
License to Operate

which had a special unit dedicated to the program. And they were trusted because they would never rat anyone out; they were just there to try to reconcile people to one another.

The point of this is that these were people who didn't live with regret. They came out of long prison terms and said, "I have to use that episode to heal my community." A Better LA saved a thousand lives in three years, according to LAPD homicide statistics. And that is the ultimate example of turning your bad life experiences into something purposeful and good.

But again, there are always people who can't look toward the future and let go of the past. For all the good that those Better LA mediators (and related organizations led by the recently deceased remarkable leader and friend, "The Commander," Dr. Aquil Basheer) did, there were plenty of their peers who couldn't move on from their old lives. They came out of prison and rejoined the gang and kept going back and back, and then they blamed society—with some justification perhaps. Their father was in jail and they were raised by a grandmother, and all of those kinds of handicaps. And it is hard to overcome that kind of background. They *do* have excuses. It just doesn't do any good to lament that. Some of them could rise above it and some couldn't.

While some of those gang members couldn't move on from the past, a lot of them did, and were successful in transforming their neighborhoods. It bears mentioning here that most readers of this book have probably never been in prison, much less belonged to a gang. So if you're buried under your past and can't move on, I have to look at those gangbangers and then look back at you, and ask, "So what's *your* excuse?"

I've got a message for anybody reading this who is going through something tough right now, whether it is a business reversal or a marriage that failed or an opportunity they missed out on—for anyone who is living in regret right now.

First, think about your big regret and address it head on. Don't try to get distracted and don't try to rationalize it. It is what it is, whether you yourself screwed up or you're a victim of somebody screwing you. It doesn't matter. *Face* it.

That doesn't mean you immediately forget about it. Maybe it's not too late. Maybe you can correct it. Maybe you can do something about it. Give it some serious thought, and then decide whether you should double down, pivot, or move on completely. Make sure you are fully in touch with your gut feelings. Take serious comfort in knowing that your response is totally up to you—that you are in control of your future actions. But you must be totally honest about what your circumstances are.

I've found that my biggest mistakes were made when I was trying to rationalize and protect my ego, as opposed to letting go of it. All successful people have had failed ventures. Or failed marriages. Or failed at *something*. But the biggest thing is to face reality. Whatever it is, accept it. Don't try to chase it down and remedy it, at least in the moment. Just accept and embrace the unchangeable facts of your life as they are—*right now*. That's the biggest thing that I've learned to do.

CHAPTER EIGHT

Have a *Defensible* Strategy

IT'S A WELL-WORN SAYING THAT THE ONLY CONSTANT IN LIFE IS change, and that's doubly true of the business world.

The late author and business consultant Clayton Christensen understood this, and his theory of "disruptive innovation," introduced in his 1997 book, *The Innovator's Dilemma*, caused quite a sensation in the business world.[9] The theory describes a pattern that replicates itself over and over: a new technology emerges, but it's expensive and/or unwieldy, so entrenched companies dismiss it as unworkable, or as a fad. But the new tech gradually becomes better and better—and also becomes cheaper as more and more people embrace it—until suddenly it isn't so fringy anymore, and those shortsighted companies that ignored it are suddenly scrambling to catch up and struggling to survive. To describe the deaths of the companies that have fallen into this trap is by now a cliché in business writing, but I'm sure you already know which companies I'm referring to: Kodak, Blockbuster, Borders, Blackberry, et al.

I get the motivation of these now-diminished or failed former business titans—they have exceptionally profitable business models and they want to protect them. But in capitalism, you can't protect a business model forever; you need to keep innovating to stay ahead. You can do this through acquisitions or Skunk Works operations or other investments, all funded by the current operation's cash flow. What you can't do is ignore trends in the marketplace and hope they go away.

Christensen's insight was that when someone devises a way to do things cheaper and more efficiently than you're doing them, that new tech ultimately wins, because your price premium gets harder and harder to justify. The upshot of this, for any entrepreneur, is that you have to constantly keep checking your rearview mirror, because there are always competitors right behind you. If you are successful, you are guaranteed to have lots of competition soon, so you have to stay ahead of the curve.

The big aha moment came for me when I became CEO of EMAK. My thinking at the time was, *Okay, you are the boss, so you need to come up with all the important strategic and visionary ideas, because that's what your job is, and that's what you're expected to do.*

But I ultimately concluded that that's actually *not* your job. Your job as CEO is to make sure that the company has a unique, compelling, and defensible advantage.

What does *defensible* mean in this context? It means, in the strategic sense, that a competitor can't easily remove you from your perch in the marketplace because you have a unique process, or unique technology, or unique talent with a unique culture, or unique client relationships. Whatever it is, you own something that makes it hard for a competitor to dislodge you from your position.

It could just be a capital advantage—if you're a company like NVIDIA, you have a multi-trillion-dollar market cap, which means you have all the intellectual and financial capital you need to keep building faster processors. It's not easy for somebody to replicate that, because it is expensive to develop, and securing funding that is reasonably priced is exceptionally difficult.

In some cases, your advantage could arise from what's called the "network effect." If you tried to start a new social media company to compete with Meta's Facebook/Instagram/What's App, you'd be at a profound disadvantage, because Meta already has a network effect—because there are so many people on it, everyone else wants to get on it, and that leaves you out in the cold, because getting people to change their habits and join something new is hard. (This is doubly true when the incumbent gives away their core service for free.) Even if someone wants to join your new platform . . . if all their friends don't do it, then they are left talking to only five people, and they quit using it. There are a few instances in which that happens. MySpace, for example, was dislodged from its dominant perch by Facebook and then Instagram. But the mix of innovation, capital, and timing that made that happen was unique.

Another defensible advantage could be your brand, and a brand advantage enables you to charge a significant price premium. Goldman Sachs is at the apex of the investment banking world, and their brand has been built over a hundred years. If you make a call with the Goldman Sachs business card, it generally will open a door. McKinsey has the same brand advantage in consulting, and it is very hard for a newcomer to establish that.

Even something like See's Candies, which was established over a century ago, has a strong brand advantage. It has deeply established distribution at Hallmark stores, pharmacy chains, and all the other places you might go to buy a box of chocolates. And the brand has nostalgic value, too. Warren Buffett thought See's Candies was a "dream business," and that's why his firm, Berkshire Hathaway, purchased the company back in 1972.[10]

Buffett was also the one who popularized the business concept of a "moat," which is pretty similar to the defensible advantage concept we're talking about here. A moat is a defensible advantage on steroids—an advantage that is practically permanent, and nearly impossible to compete with directly. A moat gives you pricing power, because the more of a moat you have, the more difficult it is for a consumer to switch from you to a different provider. So if your brand is extremely powerful, or you have some patent-protected technological edge, you can charge a premium for a long time. (All this said, there is no permanent moat in a capitalistic society, and, ultimately, like the Roman Empire, moats are vulnerable. The now ubiquitous impact of artificial intelligence on all corners of the business world will almost assuredly challenge existing moats like Google search and make it far harder to establish new moats.)

* * *

The defensible advantage concept doesn't just work in the business world. You need to know what your defensible advantage is in everyday life: to get an enviable romantic partner, a coveted job, or anything meaningful in your life.

In my personal life, in lacrosse, my defensible competitive advantage was that I was tough and fast and quick. Then, when I left sports for dancing, I had to figure it out once again: what made me stand out? Well, my prior experience playing the drums gave me a good sense of rhythm. But my real defensible advantage was teaching the steps I'd learned in New York during the emergence of the disco scene to the "backward" people of Baltimore, who hadn't yet been swept up in the disco craze. And then, when I realized that I was going to lose that edge someday, and that dancing couldn't be my lifetime calling, I had to pivot to being a very hard-working business person who had an ability to build strong teams around a commonly formed vision.

In both transitions, I jumped when I did because I realized—consciously or in my gut—the importance of having a unique, defensible advantage in life. That is the underlying reason my gut told me it was time to leave the lacrosse team: *You are going to ride the bench this year, because you've lost it. You've lost your quickness due to the multiple knee injuries, and you've lost your passion. And now, if you keep playing, you're going to be one of those mediocre players.*

That was a thought I could not abide. I mean, the passion would eventually have been lost anyway, because I wasn't ever going to be a professional lacrosse player. (Today, I believe it's possible it could have happened, but pro lacrosse didn't exist in any meaningful way in the 1970s and '80s.) Even if I had played for another year or two, it wouldn't have made any difference in the long run. Leaving the team was probably the best thing I could have done in terms of my mindset—to pivot to something

I could shine in again. (It was not the best thing I could have done for my beloved teammates, however, no matter what my role on the team would have been. Leaving that community—a brotherhood forged in the locker room and on the field—is something that still gives me pangs of regret. Fortunately, I have re-engaged with my former teammates and the overall Hopkins lacrosse program in a very meaningful way.)

You can take this mode of thinking into your personal life, too: *How do I win my ideal mate? Why should this attractive, bright lady want to be with me? Should I show her that I'm ambitious? That I'm loyal? Is my advantage that I'm courteous and kind and respectful to her? Are my looks enough to do the trick? My sense of humor? What do I have that the next guy doesn't?*

*   *   *

The best thing about devising a defensible strategy for your business is that you don't have to do it all by yourself. If the people on your management team come from different backgrounds and have different perspectives and different kinds of expertise, you can curate the best of everyone's ideas and then formulate your strategy from their input—getting their ideas and then blending them with your own. That's the job of the leader: to make sure the company *has* a compelling, defensible strategic plan and vision. It's not to do it yourself.

Look, if you are Elon Musk or Steve Jobs or somebody like that, then maybe you're smart enough to just say, "This is where we're going, and this is what we're doing. I'm smarter than all of you, I own most of the company, and your job is to implement this." But if you're not in that category of uniquely bright visionary leaders—and I am not—then your job is to recruit really smart people, let them have their voice, lead the process to put together a compelling strategic plan, and then finalize it.

The first benefit of this approach is that it is far easier to execute the plan when you have smart people contributing to it, and those people have had a say in developing it. They own it more, and they will be more motivated. Secondly, you will look good as a leader because you are really relying on your people instead of acting like a dictator. Finally—and this is particularly true when you become the leader of a bigger company—it's useful to have as many different perspectives as possible, because there are many things you might not know.

The collaborative approach doesn't mean you have to hand over your final authority; it's not a vote. You can always ignore people if their ideas aren't good ones. The CEO has to be the person who ultimately decides what we're doing, and you can always say, "I will take Cynthia's suggestion, but not Michael's."

Again, my job is not to be a visionary—because I'm *not* a visionary. I'm a smart guy, but my biggest strength is recruiting good people, letting them have a real say, and then creating an environment to let the magic happen. Critical to this is creating a culture of teamwork and inclusion, and setting up compensation programs (like bonuses and equity grants) that financially bind people to the overall performance of the company.

*   *   *

The hallmark of a defensible strategy is that it is adaptable to the inevitability of change. So if nepotism is your strategy, and you got into Yale or Harvard because you're a legacy—despite your mediocre high school GPA—well, that's not going to be sustainable when you get out into the world and your circumstances change. When you graduate from a college you never should have gotten into, all of a sudden you will find yourself competing with smarter and more talented people for jobs that they deserve more than you do—and you will be out of luck. (Perhaps your good fortune will continue if you join the family business, but eventually your lack of competence and work ethic will catch up with you.)

Or maybe your looks are the thing that opens doors for you. That's great when you're in your twenties and thirties . . . but ultimately everyone gets older, and there is always a more attractive person waiting to displace you.

Those advantages, in the long run, are not *defensible*. The best defensible advantage you can have as an individual is a strong work ethic—if you can keep it up.

Defensible advantages are more fleeting these days than they used to be because technology levels the playing field. You can outsource things you couldn't before, and quickly come up to speed. One example of this is in retail. If you're a new designer, it used to be that you had to vertically integrate and have a manufacturing capability. Now, however, you can just outsource a lot of logistics and manufacturing to a third party, and all you have to do is be a great designer. Of course, you have to understand how to price your products and everything, but the barriers to entry in most businesses are lower than they used to be.

And for most industries, no strategy is perfectly defensible. That is, you may be able to come up with a defensible strategy—you have to, if you want to survive—but you'll never be able to build a true moat.

Take advertising and marketing, for example. Because of AI and other factors, our industry is undergoing a lot of change and consolidation. Why does the world need Omelet? For us, that's the ultimate question. Would the world be worse off if we weren't there? It's a hard question to answer, and an uncomfortable one to ask, but our survival ultimately depends on our ability to answer it.

It is almost impossible for a service business to have a moat that doesn't have a network effect. Any moat we can build is apt to be fleeting—a moat filled with shallow water, with guppies instead of sharks swimming in it. So, in lieu of a moat, the best a service business can do is understand our defensible advantages and capitalize on them. And one of the best such advantages is always people. As the expression goes, in the service industry, your best assets take the elevator to the lobby at five o'clock every night.

But even the people in your organization provide a fleeting advantage that can disappear if not constantly maintained. Maybe we hired the top five account people in the field, who know every CMO in our targeted industry verticals. That's great . . . but those CMOs might change careers or retire or get fired, or maybe the people we hired oversold themselves. We hired them and paid them a fortune, and then we find that no clients actually want to follow them to work here, because Omelet is too small or because it doesn't have a New York office.

Advertising has lower barriers to entry now than it used to, because of technology like AI and editing software that is more and more accessible to people with less training and little capital. You can film an ad on an iPhone; you don't need big, expensive productions for many marketing communications that live in the digital world.

So your advantage ultimately comes down to creativity: who's got the best idea for this campaign? But someday it might no longer be you who always has the best idea, and it's relatively easy for clients to switch agencies.

There is no inherent moat. Our competitive advantage is really just doing incredible work every time, while providing impeccable client service, and even that sometimes isn't enough. Omelet is really leaning into AI, to find some unique combination of tech coupled with human judgment and experience . . . but even that advantage could be fleeting. There's always another company that's going to pick up something you don't have, so you have to keep being paranoid about your defensible advantage.

In other words, no strategy is perfectly or eternally defensible, and I don't think any company has a permanent moat these days. But simply understanding what's required is helpful, because the exercise of trying to say, "What makes us unique?" drills down to other important questions. At the very least, it helps you position yourself so you don't sound like everyone else.

*　*　*

Because disruption is inevitable, a defensible strategy is never a simple product; it has to be something that evolves with the marketplace.[11] Don't define your business by your product; define your business by the overall service and the solution that you provide—and if there's a better way to provide that service and solution, you should be indifferent to *how* you provide it, at least in theory. In advertising and marketing, an agency is in the business of measurably building a client's brand and/or driving sales growth (depending on the campaign's objectives). How an agency accomplishes that (through a TV commercial, a banner ad, a live event, print or out-of-home campaign, email marketing, et cetera) should evolve with the unique market position of your client.

Introductory marketing textbooks sometimes say that horse-and-buggy drivers should have been the inventors of the automobile because they were in the transportation business. I think that's a bit of a stretch, because the technology is so different, but the underlying point is valid: you are not in the horse-and-buggy business; you're in the business of getting from point A to point B. When automobiles began to emerge on the scene, the buggy manufacturers should have actively explored building cars—just as Kodak should have gotten into making digital cameras long before they did.

Blackberry's strategy was "email in your hand," instead of communication, generally. We all know what became of them.

Disney basically defines itself as being in the happiness business, which is smart because that leaves it room for expansion: that's why it is in the cruise ship business, and that's also why it is in home developments. If you've ever seen one of those developments, you can't help but be impressed. They're like something out of a Norman Rockwell painting: The houses have white picket fences, and there's a central town square area with a movie theater, retail stores, libraries, and everything else you would want. The houses all have porches that are designed to be neighborly and inviting.

And they cost a fortune.

Disney and others have learned when they lose sight of what business they are in, they risk impairing their brand and losing billions of dollars in market value. When Disney is laser-focused on being in the happiness business, it has no peer and merits an outsized valuation.

*　*　*

A company's values should never change. Things like telling the truth, putting team before self, acting ethically—whatever those core company values are, no matter what happens in the marketplace, that should never change. Nothing should change the essence of the company, *even if* how you manifest that essence might change in terms of the products and services you offer.

You just have to adapt to the changing marketplace and to how your consumers want to shop. Have a strategy that fits your identity, and don't try to be something you are not. At the same time, don't be limited by how you have delivered your services in the past. The mission of the company—why it exists—shouldn't change (or at least not very often). But the *strategy* to get there has to keep evolving. Most businesses used to be brick-and-mortar only, until suddenly we all had to be able to distribute online. That didn't mean our mission was suddenly different, or that the values of the company were different. We were just doing the same thing in a different, more modern, customer-focused way.

* * *

No moat is so great that you can rest on your laurels. Earlier I mentioned Kodak and Blockbuster—companies whose names have become synonymous with the term *cautionary tale* in business literature. And yet, both of those companies—and many others I haven't named—were once titans, empires whose brands were effectively moats. What's the lesson in that? That you have to keep evolving. Historically, even literal empires have not been exempt from this rule—even the Roman Empire fell eventually. Empires get complacent, they grow corrupt, and they forget to maintain whatever built them up in the first place. And then some disruptive event happens, and they vanish or become markedly diminished.

And the pace of disruption is much faster than it used to be.

* * *

Never forget the importance of properly executing your strategy. I will take a mediocre strategy flawlessly executed over a brilliant but poorly executed strategy any day of the week.

My strategy was always bust my hump, outwork the next person, and be absolutely the best I could be at whatever I did. That was what gave me my only defensible advantage. Companies can have a wide variety of defensible advantages—brand, market position, capital, network effect—but the only real, durable advantage an individual person can have is grit and resilience.

Whatever I may have had or lacked in terms of connections, intelligence, et cetera, I had grit. Few could ever outwork me. That advantage became, essentially, a moat, because I had enough drive (or insecurity—however you want to frame it) to work twenty-four hours a day, seven days a week, if that was what it took. And very few people could do that or would be willing to do that. They could be smarter than me, they could be bigger and stronger than me, but they would never be able to outwork me.

Your work ethic is the only advantage that is always totally within your control. You can't control market forces or technological advancement any more than you can control the weather, but it's hard to get out-technologied if you're outworking everyone. You can't be disrupted if your advantage is your work ethic and how you carry yourself. (Of course, you need to work smart and leverage technology like AI where appropriate, and keep focusing your grit in areas where the marketplace values your skills.)

The core lesson here is that your life situation is going to change, and your tactics need to change with it. You are going to go from analog to digital. The Wright Brothers ran a bicycle shop until they decided their future was in the air, and they pivoted from bicycles to planes. Others didn't pivot, and now they are gone. The buggy-whip guys are gone, because they saw themselves as buggy-whip guys, not as transportation guys.

I didn't have to invent my own religion to come up with a strategy built around a defensible advantage, and you don't have to invent yours either. You could get a business strategy from a consultant. You could get it from your customers. You could get it from your colleagues. It doesn't matter where it comes from. As long as you curate a good strategy, execute it flawlessly, bend with the times, and don't get caught up in movements that uproot you from your brand identity, you will almost assuredly win in the long run.

CHAPTER NINE

We, Not I

I RECENTLY WENT TO BALTIMORE FOR WHAT'S CALLED A "smoker," a longtime tradition in which former Johns Hopkins lacrosse players come back before the first home game of the season to ceremonially bestow their uniform numbers on members of the current team. There's a photo ceremony in which you take a picture with the number, and then take one with the current player who's been assigned that number. This is followed by a team update from the head coach, speeches, and a few motivational stories shared by chosen alumni. The players get pumped up by the ceremony, and the goal is for them to take that motivation and go out and win that home opening game—which they did. They beat a very good Georgetown team the next day.

Lacrosse is a very niche kind of community. It's now fully national (and international as evidenced by its inclusion in the 2028 Olympic games) and getting broader and broader, but everyone who is seriously involved with the

Hopkins Lacrosse 2025 Smoker Commemorative Mug

Bestowing jersey number 11 to current Hopkins lacrosse player
Carson Brown (second from left)

game still knows one another. I looked around at the smoker and saw seven decades of Hopkins players there—there was even somebody from one of the teams in the 1940s—and of course, all the current players.

In recent years, I've become much more involved with the Hopkins lacrosse program. I'm one of the lead player mentors, and I have gotten close with the coaches. Every year, the players from my era—the mid-1970s to the early '80s—go away for four days to the Eastern Shore of Maryland and Delaware to hang out.

It's very special to be part of that community. To play at that level, on a national championship team (Hopkins has forty-four national

Annual reunion: Hopkins lacrosse players from the mid-1970s to early 1980s,
Bethany Beach, Delaware (fourth from left on couch)

championships since beginning varsity play in 1883), is something that not many people can say they've done. I'm proud to be part of that fraternity, and I'm proud of the contributions I have made both on and off the field. The camaraderie and the bonds formed by teamwork are like nothing else you'll ever experience.

And speaking of teamwork, let's dive into the real subject of this chapter.

* * *

One of the best aspects of being part of a team is the shared joy in victory—the shared sense of purpose. As a member of a team, you can have a great game personally—scoring a lot of points and demonstrating your value as an individual—and still feel that your accomplishments are meaningless if your team doesn't win the game. You always hear these guys interviewed after a game—the quarterback breaks a record, but they lose anyway, and afterward, he says, "I don't care about my stats. We lost. All I want to do is win the championship."

I don't know if all of them really believe that 100 percent when they say it (it has to feel good to break a record, doesn't it?), but I think there's a lot of truth in the sentiment. And that's why I try to foster that sense of *team* in the companies I have run.

There's a lot of joy to go around when you celebrate a win with others, and it's a joy you can only experience in a team effort. I'm sure if you win the US Open Tennis Championship, you have coaches and family members to share the joy of your victory. They are all happy *for* you—but it is still your win or your loss.

In contrast, watch how the winning team behaves at the end of a Super Bowl, or Game 7 of the World Series. They jump up and down in the middle of a giant group hug, or they pour Gatorade over the coach's head. Each player is far prouder of his contribution to the team's win than he would have been of a mere statistical achievement. There's joy in winning either way, of course, but I far prefer the team sport experience.

Have you ever seen the war movie, *Full Metal Jacket*? The drill sergeant, Hartman, gives every one of the Marine recruits in his charge a nickname, and he dubs one particularly dimwitted recruit "Private Pyle," after the pea-brained Marine in the eponymous TV sitcom, *Gomer Pyle, USMC*. One day, during a barracks inspection, he finds that Private Pyle has taken a jelly donut from the mess hall and stored it in his footlocker—which is *not* allowed. So he makes Pyle eat that donut in the middle of the barracks while the rest of his platoon has to do pushups for the entire scene. He then institutes a collective punishment policy, under which the entire platoon will be punished every time Pyle screws up. And because Pyle screws up and everyone else on the team has to pay for it, they end up beating the daylights out of him to make sure it doesn't happen again.

It's a grim scene in a grim movie, but there's actually something beautiful underlying those Marines' motivations: a sense of shared destiny. I like that. When that sense of shared destiny is applied to something in the civilian world—like a sports team or a business enterprise—it makes things more fun and more celebratory.

On the day of that early February game against Georgetown, it was 32 degrees and hailing . . . and the players on the sidelines were sitting there on the bench, shivering in their game shorts because they wouldn't put on parkas. Why? Because nobody else on the team was wearing them—the players on the field didn't have them, so nobody would wear them. We're on a team, and whether you're running around on the field or sitting on the bench waiting to play, we're all the same. And everyone's uniform appearance needs to be exactly the same. Some don't wear ankle socks while others wear tube socks—they all wear the same type of socks. The starters aren't wearing parkas, so nobody else will wear one, either. It's damned cold sitting on the sidelines, particularly in your shorts, but with that act of solidarity, you end up making the team better. And it's a truly selfless person who can perform that act.

People who subscribe to this philosophy are my ideal business partners and employees.

* * *

Successful people are often successful because their peers hold them to high standards. And this is as true on the best athletic teams as it is in military service. Bill Belichick, the famous New England Patriots coach (and now head coach at the University of North Carolina), was famous for saying, "Do your job." If each guy does his job, things are going to work out—and implied in that is the understanding that you are relying on your teammates to do *their* jobs.

In team sports, the weakest link is generally where teams lose, so when you get to a point where you don't want to let your teammates down, that becomes your motivation. The French call this sense of group solidarity *esprit de corps*. There's nothing worse than being the reason your team lost— and of course, in the military, if you don't do your job, somebody could die.

In any team situation, there is a passion for personal integrity that comes from making your commitment to the team. You owe it to the team to do your job really well, and it's understood that you have every expectation that they will do theirs. On a sports team, this means you work hard in practice and you don't slack off; in a business setting, it means you are on time and fully prepared for meetings. Either way, it's part of the commitment. And that's why I like to hire athletes and veterans, honestly—they already have that foundation of discipline and commitment to the team.

* * *

Here's how the Private Pyle Principle works at Omelet: Before we start an assignment, the strategy department writes a creative brief, which basically says, *This is what the client is looking for, this is who their target market is and who their key competitors are, this is the essence of what we have to do, and these are the key metrics for success.* If the strategy department puts together a bad brief, the creatives will be screwed when they go to start the project, because the creatives need guidelines—they can't just start coming up with stuff out of thin air. So if that brief is not good, then the whole thing is going to fall apart.

A team sport is a great way to prepare someone for this kind of culture. In the preseason and during training camp, you're competing with your teammates to get a starting spot—who is going to be the starting goalie? Those competitions can get very heated, and if the coach didn't choose you to start, but you think you were better than someone else who *was* chosen, there can be some resentment. At Hopkins, for example, pretty much everyone on the roster was a high school star—and now, all of a sudden they are sitting on the bench, and many of them don't think they should be.

One of the guys who spoke at a recent smoker, the great lacrosse goalie Larry Quinn,[12] didn't start for the first two years of his career, and then he was a first-team All-American in the two years he started. Quinn was very good as a freshman and as a sophomore, but he didn't get to start because there was a senior ahead of him. As Quinn recounted after the fact at the smoker, he was kind of disgruntled until one of the coaches took him aside and said, in substance, "Every practice is an audition to win the starting job, but *your* job today is to compete at the highest possible level. That's what your job is. And then, by doing so, either you are going to win the starting job, or you are going to make the starter that much better because he's really worried about you taking his starting position away from him."

Quinn took that message to heart, and he went on to become, some people will say, the best goalie of all time. It took him a long time, but he accepted that role. You have to have pride and accept your role in order to be a great teammate. Really good teammates push the starters in practice and encourage them to perform well enough to keep their roles; that's their job. Whatever game you're playing, everyone on the team needs to say to themselves, *You know what? My role—my job—is to be the best left fielder or long snapper I can possibly be, and if I do my job really well, my teammates are going to be more confident and more effective in their roles, and maybe that makes the difference between winning and losing.*

The same spirit that makes the US Marine Corps or the New England Patriots effective works in the business world. If you work for me, I want you to never look for credit yourself. I've never liked to hire ego-driven superstars, even though they are talented. Creative businesses are famously rife with prima donnas, but I would rather have honest, solid team players who subordinate themselves to the team and the greater good. That ethos has permeated all the companies I've run.

But doesn't everybody *want* superstars? No. You want the superstar *capability*, but not the ego. Superstars can sometimes not be good teammates, because they get frustrated if somebody is slower or less effective than they are. They are also quick to jump to the next job if they get a higher offer. They look to get credit for everything they do, which is a frustrating thing in a team-based environment. One of the core values of Omelet is *We, Not I*. Everyone, no matter how good they are, has to remember that it's not about who gets the credit; it's about the success of the company. The idea is that you don't care who had the idea.

This isn't just a warm and fuzzy concept. It reflects reality. A great creative idea that isn't fully developed with multiple executions in multiple media won't cut it. And a great idea that isn't flawlessly produced on time and on budget is essentially worthless, so the entire team needs to execute that great idea in order for the client to have a big success.

Superstars also present a problem when it comes to compensation. If someone is a super salesperson, you can give them commissions, and that person can get rich . . . even though they partly depend on others to close the sale. This is analogous to the hypothetical football player I mentioned earlier, who has such a great individual game that he breaks a record—and yet his team loses.

One way to address this is with a compensation structure that provides bonuses based on overall company results—so even if you personally had a really good year, you wouldn't get a bonus (or your bonus would be very small) because the team didn't hit its goals. This incentivizes everyone not to be the reason the high performers didn't get their bonuses—i.e., not to be the reason the team lost the game. No one wants to get beaten up like Private Pyle.

* * *

I am going to touch on a concept that is a sensitive one for some, but I think it is critically important to address.

In recent decades, and especially in recent years, our culture has become obsessed with the concept of *diversity*—which is a wonderful thing, if the concept is properly understood. Many people think of diversity in terms of skin color, sexuality, religion, or some other identity characteristic, but what's really important from a business standpoint is diversity of *perspective*.

The reason to promote diversity in a company is to become a better company, and you only become a better company if you have the perspectives of a broader team. You have perspectives in a brainstorm that might be different than those you'd have if everyone on the team grew up in exactly the same environment and thought the same way. That kind of diversity gives you a richer mix of potentially valuable opinions, which is vital for a creative company, and for most businesses that have to deal with the general public.

In order to get diversity of perspective, you need diversity of thought. Skin color or gender or religion *can* be a factor that makes you think differently . . . but it might not. Hire and promote people based on their character and their capabilities and the way they think, and you will build a great company. Source candidates from a broad pool, including outside the traditional industry pipelines, and in my experience, you will end up with a demographically diverse team, because there are fabulously talented people of all races and genders and religions and family income levels. But your "true north" is to hire and promote the best possible people, and then the diversity takes care of itself.

*   *   *

Modern technology has made it possible for 35 percent of us to work from home[13] . . . and since the Covid-19 pandemic, far too many of us are doing so. Working from home may seem like a luxury that improves people's lives, but in my view, it undermines team cohesion and organizational effectiveness.

Los Angeles, where Omelet is based, is by far the most work-from-home place in the country, partly because so many people have moved away from the city proper in the past twenty years because they couldn't afford homes there. But working from home, while it may seem efficient (no more hour-long commute on the 405 Freeway!), is just not the same. When you actually come into the office, the quality of your work is often better, you learn how to interact with people, and you generally develop your character far better than you would have done sitting at home. I spent the whole early part of my career going out with people virtually every night after work—going out for drinks, going out for dinner, et cetera. Besides being fun, that kind of socialization forms bonds of trust among professional colleagues—bonds that go a long way toward minimizing conflicts and encouraging people to sublimate their egos.

I think some people today just don't get—or have forgotten—the joy of teams. The whole human dynamic seems to have changed for younger people, particularly those who ended up taking remote classes in college, thanks to Covid. They don't seem to be as well-adjusted as people who are even just a few years older than they are, and it's incredible to me that they wouldn't want to go to the office every day—to see their boss, to go out with colleagues for lunch and after work, and to interact with people on a spontaneous, one-to-one basis.

Maybe you can sneak an opportunity to do your laundry at home, and you couldn't do that if you were in the office, and of course you save time and money on the commute you don't have to make every day . . . but those are really small-ball things. The trade-offs, in terms of the loss of the benefits of face-to-face interaction, are not worth it. If Marines were given the option to take basic training from home, can you imagine them growing into the kind of Marines their brothers-in-arms could depend on?

But because these younger people were at the start of their careers when this work-from-home explosion happened, they just don't know any better. Those who aren't allowed to work from home agitate for the right to do so, and those who do work from home sometimes complain if they're asked to come into the office several days per week. Because of this, some companies are now saying, "If you want to work here, you have to come to the office. If you don't want to come to the office, then fine, I respect that, but you cannot work here."

At the root of this work-from-home problem, of course, is technology—specifically screen technology, and more specifically, people's phones. Another hindrance to teams, and a major contributor to the deep political divisions we see today, is the way we communicate. People have become unwilling to date or do business with people who have different political views, and this is all exacerbated by social media. Technology can isolate people and make it harder to form effective teams at work. Unfortunately, an entire generation of young adults has grown up never having experienced life without a phone in their faces all day.

At the risk of sounding like a cranky old guy, my generation—and the generation that came after us—*played outside* as kids. Yes, we watched a lot of television, but we weren't on screens ten hours a day. And I think that face-to-face interaction with real people in the physical world built up our ability to interface with one another and work out our problems. You had the bully in the neighborhood, and you also had the kid who was not a great athlete and didn't get picked for the flag football team in gym class. There were jocks and class presidents and bullies and nerds and hippies and weirdos, and we all had to get along with one another and come to mutual understanding in order to solve whatever problems we had.

That skill, if you're able to acquire it as a child, becomes invaluable in adult life. The messiness of dealing with people is a reality you have to learn, and my generation had no other choice. And because we had to learn this foundational social skill, I think we were mentally healthier and better off in general. I don't have kids, but my understanding is that there is now so much focus on the phone, on social media interactions, and on keeping pace with friends, that teenagers become riddled with anxiety and other psychological disorders. More and more then get prescribed medication to deal with the issues, which leads to an entirely new set of problems.

The problem has now spread to the adult world as well. I'm fascinated when I see people on vacation and all they do is take selfies, not even engaging with the Eiffel Tower or whatever landmark they're visiting. All they seem to think is, *Oh my God, this will be a great Instagram post, with me acting like I'm having a great time!*

Yeah, I know—who am I to judge, or to say how they should be enjoying their vacation? If that's what they want to do at the Eiffel Tower, let them do it. It does bother me, though, and I feel sad for them. Posting envy porn online seems like the only way they know to get respect, and when they enter the workforce, they don't learn to cooperate and negotiate with others. A kind of socialization that once existed is gone now, and as a result, it is harder for people to coalesce and to form teams.

If you pay attention to the news—regardless of where you get it—you're surely aware that Americans feel a level of hostility toward one another that hasn't been seen since at least the 1960s . . . and perhaps not since the Civil War. Well, maybe our society is so polarized because people aren't out with all kinds of *other* types of people, playing and working and just learning to get along, including respecting people's differences. I absolutely believe that people with different political views than mine can be intelligent, decent, empathetic, and kind. I am often baffled by their views, but I do not judge them. Some of my closest friends, business associates, and family members have different political views than I do, and that is totally cool.

Social media algorithms feed you a picture of the world based on whatever your tribe is. You get the dopamine hit of curated outrage, and in return, they get your invaluable personal data. (Does that sound like a fair trade to you?) If you are into politics and you are a Republican, you are going to see Elon Musk and Donald Trump-related content; if you are a Democrat, you'll see content from Kamala Harris or my former Hopkins board colleague and friend Governor Wes Moore of Maryland. Either way, most of what you see is demonizing the other side.

I don't think it's a huge stretch to say that this kind of polarization starts when kids are not out interfacing with other kids. They are just in their own worlds, on their own devices, seeing only what they want to look at and what they are being fed in their feeds.

* * *

How do you create a sense of team today? First, you need to have a shared vision that everyone signs up for—an ambition to be the greatest creative company in the world, or whatever that true north is that everyone must be committed to in your organization. And when I say *committed*, I mean being all-in, not just going through the motions.

Secondly, you build a brand that people are proud to work for. If you are a consultant, there is a certain badge of honor in being able to tell people you work for McKinsey. The same is true for Goldman Sachs in investment banking, or for any organization widely regarded as superior in its field—and people *want* that brand association.

In other words, your first concern is how you attract and retain the right types of people. Equally important is the need to exit those people who are not performing and/or are not living the company's values.

I once read a piece in *Harvard Business Review* that described a four-box matrix, divided along two axes, cultural fit, and performance, with a different employee type in each box. In the top-left corner is the first employee type: he or she is a great performer *and* a great cultural fit—meaning that they consciously embrace the values of the company. Obviously, you retain that person and promote them and do everything you can to keep them.

In the lower-right corner is the second employee type: a lousy performer who is also a bad cultural fit. Not a lot of debate that you get rid of *that* guy, and you do it very quickly. He is disruptive, *and* he is not good at his job.

The third employee type is in the lower-left corner: not a great performer, but is a great cultural fit. Those are the people you invest in and try to bring up to speed if you can, because they work their asses off, they are good team players, and people like them. Ultimately, if they don't cut it, you have to move on, but you have to at least *try* to keep people like that.

The key question for a manager is . . . how do you treat that last box? The first three boxes are obvious, but look at the last, top-right box: the high performer who is a bad cultural fit. They don't give credit for the good work of their colleagues. They don't mentor anyone. They come in late. They tend to be cynical, and they are often the Eddie Haskells of the organization, sucking up to you and anyone else who can help them get ahead: "Hello, Mrs. Cleaver, that's a lovely dress you have on!"

And as soon as the person he's sucking up to leaves, he bad-mouths them.

Do you have the necessary conviction to fire a star performer because they are disruptive to the team? I struggle with this issue like everyone does, because you can't help thinking, *Damn, she is* really *good at her job.* But I have nevertheless terminated a number of those people in my career, and I'm proud to have done so. Again, this is what you have to do to make sure the team, and not the individual, is paramount.

It's hard, and the way I get the nerve to do it is by reminding myself that if I don't fire them I will lose respect from the rest of the company, because it's obvious we're making an exception to the rules for a superstar. It's obvious that they don't have to live by the same values the rest of us do. And that feeling of not being looked up to as a good leader who walks the talk—the loss of respect—is a very powerful motivator. And that will get me to act.

* * *

So, to sum it all up: Working as part of a good team, one that operates like a well-oiled machine, is the most rewarding professional experience you'll ever have. When you're bound to teammates by a sense of shared destiny, you share the joy of victory in a way that magnifies it—and you still have support when things don't go as well.

In order to maintain the effectiveness of your team, everyone on it must feel highly motivated not to be the one who lets the team down, and any team member who cannot or will not embrace this ethos has to be let go. No member of the team can be allowed to make his or her ego the team's central concern, even if he or she is a superstar—remember, it's *We, Not I.*

And if that egocentric person is abusive toward his or her coworkers, it is even more imperative that they be quickly let go—even though, as we'll see in the next chapter, their abusive behavior says more about them than it says about anyone else.

CHAPTER TEN

When People Say Stupid, Hurtful Things, It's About Them—Not You

YEARS AGO, I WAS APPROACHED BY SOMEBODY WITH SOME MONEY who wanted me to run for Congress. "You should run," they said, and while I was flattered, I thought to myself, *I would never be able to take the negative campaigning stuff*. I probably wouldn't have done it anyway, but that prospect was the dealbreaker for me.

You've seen how most political campaigns are run—the lies and the vicious attacks on the opposing candidate's character. I could picture the attack ads, with their low, ominous-sounding voiceovers: "Don Kurz wants to take your health insurance and social security away, and may very well have a financial conflict of interest in alternatives to these programs."

It's always like that. They lie and lie, and there is nothing you can do. I knew I didn't have the thick skin needed to be a politician.

I still don't have that thick skin today . . . but I *really* didn't have it back then. For most of my life, I cared intensely about what other people thought—but I don't anymore. I've undergone a transformation in my thinking over the past few years.

When people are too dependent on the good opinions of others, they become frozen. They are no longer able to act in the world in a way that advances their own interests. On the other hand, when people don't pay *enough* attention to others, they might get a reputation as an egotist, or even a sociopath. Thankfully, there is a sweet spot.

The question is . . . how much do you *really* need to be liked in life?

Trying to get everyone to like you is futile. It is the ultimate game of whack-a-mole—the more you do to please one type of acquaintance, the more you will upset another. It's an impossible quest. Once you start to become successful—once you make more money than others, or get into a better college, or are the starting midfielder and they are not, or get promoted at work faster than your peers—jealousy and envy make their appearance. People can be very mean, and they will attribute your success to anything but your actual virtues: "Of course you got that promotion—you suck up to the boss!"

And even if they admit that you earned what you have on the basis of merit, they'll *still* be bitter: "Okay, you earned it fair and square . . . but now you're in management, so screw you. You are now one of *them*."

*　*　*

I used to try to make people like me at (nearly) any cost. One reason I am good at selling is that I am very good at reading what's in people's minds, and I can instinctively feed back to you what I know you are going to want to hear. I can be the jock, I can be the dancer, or I can be the smart guy. I can be gregarious or I can be quiet. I am constantly reading and delivering back what I think is going to be effective. I was always good at selling myself, and I had a relatively easy time getting along with a wide variety of people. (I do want to note that this trait of instinctively selling was not something I was conscious of until well into my adult life. It is just something I subconsciously did.) This approach is an effective way to deal with people, but it can become a problem if you start compromising yourself and become too much of a chameleon. You hang out with the jocks and then you hang out with the druggies and then you hang out with the nerds

. . . and eventually you don't really know who you are. (I don't believe I fell into that trap, as I truly enjoyed socializing with a wide variety of folks, but clearly there is a delicate balance.)

An interesting illustration of this is back in the late '80s, in my days of working for a major management consulting firm (now part of global behemoth Willis Towers Watson), a guy I worked with didn't seem to like me very much. We were in the flagship New York office together on the renowned corporate row of Park Avenue—he was a manager, and I was a supervisory consultant. He was one level above me, and he knew that the big boss liked me, and that I was on a fast track, so he was mean to me. He wouldn't give me the time of day, no matter what, and that bothered me because he was relatively popular. He was a big guy, likeable, and good with the ladies. He was *cool*.

But he wasn't exceptionally smart or motivated, which is probably why my career was moving faster than his. I think he didn't like me because I was threatening to him. So to get this guy to like me, after trying every other tactic, I acted like he didn't even exist. There wasn't ever any kind of blowup; I just didn't notice him . . . and then he started being really nice to me and subsequently became a very good friend. Go figure.

* * *

Here's another example of my lifelong drive to be liked. When I was eleven years old, I was in Pop Warner Football, playing for the Elmont Cardinals. I was always a relatively little guy, small for my age, and we played in a very tough league—those other kids were *big*. In addition to an age restriction (I believe up to age thirteen), there was a maximum weight for the players—130 pounds—so in order to qualify, players who weighed closer to 140 would eat less and then not drink water before their annual weigh-in. Then, after the weigh-in, they would eat as much as they wanted for the rest of the season, with some playing during the season at close to 150 pounds. (They also sometimes grew an inch or two during the four months of the season.)

I weighed ninety-two pounds with all my clothes on.

Plus, we had a terrible team. We lost multiple games by eighty or more to nothing. (I remember two 80–0 games against Massapequa and Huntington.) There was no mercy rule during that era. I'm not sure we even scored one point the entire season. There also wasn't a big concern about concussions back then, and the hitting was fierce—you tackled with your head, and helmet-to-helmet contact was celebrated.

I started as a running back, but it turned out that we had a problem selecting a quarterback. Nobody else wanted to play that position because there was no effective blocking (because the team was terrible), so the quarterback would repeatedly get clobbered.

The coach (a hard-drinking, foul-mouthed, old-school guy named Buddy Burke) didn't even want me, a small kid, to go out for the team when he first saw me; he needed big, tough kids because we were in the top Pop Warner division on Long Island. But *because* I had always been on the small side, I always felt I had to prove myself.

So I ended up being the quarterback, and as my coach eventually acknowledged, I was fearless. At the end of the season, I was selected for the league's all-star team (each team had to have at least one player on the all-star team). I remember that when they introduced me at the awards banquet, they focused not on my skills, but on how I took a beating each game yet never gave up.

Why did I drive myself so hard at football? Well, I certainly was passionate about the game, but it was also part of my never-ending quest to be popular and well-liked. Of course, by the time I grew up, I knew intellectually that this was not a good thing, and that to be liked by everyone was an impossible task. But knowing something

*In Elmont Cardinal uniform with
brother Mitch in background*

intellectually and really *feeling* it are not the same thing, are they? It's like when a romantic partner dumps you for someone else—you know you shouldn't be stuck on this lady who left you, because you know she isn't coming back, and you know intellectually that you need to move on . . . but you just *can't*.

It's impossible to make someone love you and want you if they don't, and in the same way, it's impossible to make someone like you or admire you or want to be your friend if they're just not interested. And yet many people try to do this, at least some of the time. And some people try all the time—with disappointing results.

I don't want to suggest I spent every waking moment thinking about what everyone thought of me, but it was often in the back of my mind; instinctively, I wanted to get people to really like me.

I don't do that anymore. I don't know what triggered the change, but one day my general anxiety just lowered—a lot. It took me decades to learn not to do it, but I don't drive myself crazy that way anymore. If you and I have a phone call and you hang up and go tell your spouse, "That guy is the biggest schmuck I've ever met," and I find out . . . well, it's not like I'm going to *like* it. And it's not even that I won't care. I *will* care. I just won't obsess over it, and I won't try to fix something that doesn't really need to be fixed.

Letting go of that perpetual concern released a lot of energy, and I wish I'd figured this out decades earlier than I did, because it's really draining to worry so much about your standing with the entire world. It is *exhausting*, constantly trying to manage that problem. Worse, it is not productive. If you know you can't win, then maybe you shouldn't be playing the game.

Fortunately, while the desire to be liked may have caused me some anxiety, it ultimately didn't rule me—because while I was very outgoing, I was even more *ambitious*. And ambition is inherently incompatible with the project of making oneself universally loved. You want to get everyone to like you? I can give you one surefire way: don't succeed. Don't take their sales deal away from them. Don't take their starting position on the team. Don't take their girlfriend. Don't take the promotion they're hoping for.

That's great life advice, isn't it? *Don't succeed.* But . . . is that really how you want to live your life?

It sure wasn't how I wanted to live mine. I wanted to be successful, and my quest to succeed outweighed and overwhelmed the need to be liked. The need was still there, of course, but it didn't stop my pursuit of the good life—it just made the journey more unpleasant.

But I could handle a little unpleasantness. I would not hold back my own drive for success because of some irrational fear that my success might come at the expense of someone else, or that they might not like me because I'd succeeded where they failed. As long as I competed ethically and didn't undermine anyone, I was very comfortable climbing the career and sports ladders.

*   *   *

The drive to make ourselves liked at all costs isn't healthy, but it is human. We all do this to some degree, and there are lots of reasons for it.

A feeling of safety is one reason. I would pleasantly engage with everyone I came in contact with, but I was particularly focused on people whose goodwill I was dependent on for my well-being. Even today, I'm very friendly with all my doctors, for example. They hold my life in their hands, after all. Before going into surgery, you want that surgeon to *care* about you. Not that they are going to deliberately harm you because they don't like you ("Whoops, sorry, dude, I cut your leg off instead of pulling your tonsils out"), but there is no downside in them caring about you personally. (All that said, I have been fortunate to have wonderful doctors whom I genuinely want to be friends with.)

More than anything else, though, I think the main reason we all do this is that we're human beings and we crave connection. Winning other people's approval reduces social friction and makes it easier to make real connections, and *that's* the value of it. Besides, I don't think anyone *likes* not being liked, particularly if we feel that the other person's negative opinion is unjust.

But there comes a certain point in your life when you just have to realize that you are who you are, and you accept who you are. Whether it is your sexual orientation, your ability to be monogamous and stay in a committed relationship like marriage, or your desire to pursue the arts instead of the career your parents are pushing you into—at some point, no matter the consequences, you have to be true to yourself. Repressing reality has enormous physical and emotional consequences you cannot escape. Unhappy married couples, for example, can be forced into a state of acceptance . . . until in the long run, the marriage blows up because one partner or the other can't pretend anymore.

What you ultimately need, instead of being liked, is people's respect. And you get that respect not just by succeeding, but also by acting ethically and not undermining people through your success. They might not like you, but grudgingly they will come to respect you, and that is really all you can hope for. As long as you behave in a manner you can be proud of in hindsight, you can go to sleep at night knowing you've been honest with the world, and that satisfaction should overwhelm any feeling of not being liked.

In sports or in business, you can win people's respect by being a really good teammate. That worked for me as a kid playing Pop Warner football, and it worked again when I played lacrosse at Hopkins. I was a

25th anniversary celebration of 1974 Hopkins NCAA Championship team at the University of Maryland's Byrd Stadium, College Park, Maryland (front row, center, in white t-shirt)

50th anniversary celebration of 1974 Hopkins NCAA Championship team at Johns Hopkins Homewood Field, Baltimore, Maryland (I'm tipping my hat in the center)

freshman on a very senior-heavy team that had lost the national championship game two years in a row, the last one by one goal. So when I came in and earned one of the top midfield slots, there was some resentment, and everyone on the team probably didn't like me right away. That took quite a while, but I didn't do anything special to further that goal, other than playing really hard. Eventually, it became clear that I'd earned the spot, and I got respect for it.

And once I had their respect, being liked followed on its own. And to this day, I remain very friendly with all the players on that team.

Today, I don't worry about it like I did back then. Of course, I don't want people *not* to like me, but I'm not going to go out of my way to try to manage their feelings. It's impossible, particularly if you are successful. I still sometimes encounter people who don't like me because they don't think I've earned what I have, or they are jealous, but at some point in my life, I just stopped trying to correct it. That freed up a lot of emotional energy. I am now far more at peace than I have ever been.

My father, who recently passed at 101 years of age, always said there are two buckets into which you can put everything in life. Bucket number one is *things you can control*, and those are the things you should spend your time on. Bucket two is *things you can't control*, and that bucket should get not a single minute of your time. When you recognize that something belongs in bucket number two, just leave it. Do not obsess over it, because you really can't do anything about it. And take comfort in that, because it's one less thing you have on your plate.

Other people's opinion of you is something you can't control. That goes in bucket number two. What you *can* control is how you act toward people—and their response to you is out of your hands.

Sometimes people conjure up an image of you as the villain because they don't want to acknowledge their own failures, and they will ascribe to you some negative trait you don't have or blame you for something you didn't do. I lost that childhood friend over paying him for making an introductory phone call. I'm certain that to this day, that guy thinks I screwed him over. But there's nothing I can do about that—he'll just think whatever he's going to think. I am now fully at peace with it, and I hope he is, too.

As you go through life, you will encounter lots of people who expect you to be something other than what you are, or who expect things from you that they're not entitled to; those people will most likely end up disliking you in the long run.

And you have to live with that. You just say, "Okay, I guess that's how it is," and you go on. You have to, because the alternative is a lot of anxiety. And there is no path out of that anxiety other than to accept the reality of human connection and human nature. This acceptance and embracing of reality is a far better solution than taking Xanax.

CHAPTER ELEVEN

Life Has Too Many Variables:
You Can't Control Everything—So Don't Even Try

I DON'T GO CAMPING VERY OFTEN; I DON'T EVEN KNOW HOW TO pitch a tent. I've tried, though, and if you've ever struggled with that project, you know how it goes—you put a stake in the ground at one end, you knock it in, and you go to the other side and repeat the process . . . and it pops the other one out. And round and round you go until you finally say, "To hell with this, we're going to a hotel tonight!"

Now that I've outed myself as an indoorsman, those of you who are camping enthusiasts are probably having a good laugh at my expense. But if you've ever had a similarly frustrating experience, it may have struck you as a metaphor for the impossible task of managing the relentless, unpredictable stream of curve balls that life throws at us every day.

In previous chapters, I've advocated an "accept and embrace" approach to life's challenges and setbacks. And one thing I've learned from accepting and embracing is that life is what mathematicians call a multivariate equation.

If you don't recall your eighth-grade algebra too well, a *univariate* equation is simple because it has only one variable: for example 2 + x = 5 is simple enough for a seven-year-old to solve. But a *multivariate* equation like 2x + 3y − z = 7 can make your brain hurt if you don't have a natural talent for math.

How is this relevant to your everyday life? If you invest a lot of time and mental bandwidth in trying to control your environment—particularly your *external* environment—then you are setting yourself up for a lifetime of frustration, disappointment, and nasty surprises.

I'm in a client service business, and clients often do things you don't expect, sometimes very abruptly. In my business, everything is great until your biggest client gets fired or leaves their job, or a new CEO is brought in with allegiance to a different advertising agency—and then, all of a sudden, you're out on an island, stranded and starving.

When something like that happens, you have to resist the temptation to fight it for two reasons. One, because it is out of your control. And two . . . it *happened*. When an adverse event occurs, you have to accept the reality of it, and then figure out what you can do immediately to mitigate it. In a case like the one I described above, that may mean something as simple as asking your client to give a great recommendation to their successor. Whatever it is, you just have to do the best you can and start looking for other complementary pieces of business, while simultaneously taking a hard look at your cost structure. It just is the way it is. By all means, learn whatever lessons you can from the situation, but your full focus should be on how best to move forward.

As I noted in the previous chapter, my father, may he rest in peace, always said to put life into two buckets: things you can control and things you can't. You have to do your best to control the things you can—your emotions, how you react to setbacks, how hard you work, how well prepared you are, et cetera—and accept the things you can't.

It's a bit like the Serenity Prayer popularized by Alcoholics Anonymous: "God, grant me the serenity to accept the things I cannot change, the courage to change the things I can, and the wisdom to know the difference."[14]

*　*　*

When an adverse situation develops in your life, just be as aware of it as you can be, without fixating on changing or reversing the unwelcome development. It's not a matter of ignoring it; just accept it: *Wow, I don't have my relationship with that client anymore*, or *Damn, my girlfriend has decided she has had it with me*. Maybe your kid just got suspended from school for three days. You can't ignore that. It *happened* . . . so now what are you going to do? How are you going to deal with it?

You can't fight what happens, because it doesn't do any good. Life is not fair. It is not fair that your best client has left you sitting out on an island when you were doing great work for them. But all you can do is try to be as serene as possible, leaning into the brutal reality of the situation rather than trying to escape from it. Respond to what you can control, and have faith that as long as you are doing your part in life, things will work out. My experience has been that adverse situations invariably lead to long-term favorable outcomes, as long as you do your part by working hard and conducting yourself with integrity.

And that's something that took me a long time to learn, because it is frustrating when things happen that are out of your control when you think you are doing everything right. Just recently, I was on my way to physical therapy at 8:30 a.m. on a weekday, during a nasty winter storm with freezing rain pouring down, when my car suddenly went into an uncontrollable skid in the middle of a very busy intersection on Franklin Road in Nashville. I was approaching a red light, so any car coming the other way would have had a green light and would not have slowed down. For several agonizing seconds, I white-knuckled the steering wheel, skidding into the intersection, certain that I was going to get hit and end up in the hospital again. (I had been in physical therapy recovering from extensive spine surgery.)

Fortunately I wasn't injured, nor was anyone else. I remembered to give the car a little gas and I straightened out. I hate to think what would have happened if anyone had been coming the other way, but if that was my fate, I would have had to accept it. I'm not saying I'd be sitting there in the emergency room serenely, but in retrospect, I couldn't have done anything differently. I was going slow. I was in a low gear. I was doing everything that an experienced, careful driver should be expected to do. But it happened anyway.

I was just very lucky; I didn't get hit, even though my car was right in the middle of a busy intersection at the height of rush hour. And that's how life is: sometimes you get lucky, and other times, it is your turn to get a bad break.

*　*　*

When you do get a bad break, it's important not to catastrophize. Bad luck is inevitable, and you can't let it destroy your confidence or your ability to respond. Life will sometimes dish out devastating body blows, and if you want to be able to absorb them, you may want to heed the example of one of the greatest fighters of all time (or *The* Greatest, if you were to ask him): Muhammad Ali.

Ali deliberately allowed himself to get pummeled in the ring, an unusual strategy he called "rope-a-dope": you assume a defensive posture—protecting your head and face—and lean back against the ropes, tricking your opponent into thinking you're in trouble (i.e., "on the ropes"). Then you stay there and take whatever punishment he gives you, counting on the elasticity of the ropes themselves to absorb some of the impact of the blows, and you wait for him to tire himself out—and that's when you go on the offensive.

It's a great strategy . . . but it's not easy. Even with your face protected by your gloves, and even with the ropes helping your body absorb the punishment, getting pounded by the likes of George Foreman in his prime was no day at the beach.

But Ali took it. During his 1974 title fight with Foreman in Zaire, the "Rumble in the Jungle," he sucked it up and persevered while spectators worried that he might actually be killed in the ring. Foreman had been undefeated and was heavily favored, but in the eighth round, Ali suddenly came alive and stunned Foreman with a series of quick, powerful punches, knocking him out and reclaiming the heavyweight championship of the world.

Ali's victory came at a cost—he had to absorb a lot of punishment to wear Foreman out—but it also required careful strategizing beforehand. Foreman was the stronger of the two fighters, whereas Ali's speed was considered his best asset. Ali knew that Foreman could wear him down if he allowed him to, by forcing Ali to constantly dodge his blows, taking two steps for every step Foreman took. So he came up with a plan.

What Ali did *not* do was freak out at the prospect of fighting an opponent who had steamrolled every fighter he faced. Instead, he came up with a bold strategy and stepped into the ring determined to give it his all and shock the world.

If you're in Ali's position before that fight, you can't control the variables: the weather, the referee, the crowd, the time of night (the fight took place at 4:00 a.m. so that it could be shown on US television at 10:00 p.m.), or the strength of your opponent.

But you *can* control your strategy and your willingness to take a beating in the service of that strategy. If you just resign yourself to taking a pummeling—and it is not going to be pleasant, but you know you *can* take it because you trained relentlessly in support of this strategy—then you can outlast your opponent.

Likewise, if you can resign yourself to accepting life's body blows before they hit you, then you are going to outlast all the negativity that anyone can throw your way. You can choose not to engage with people who are fighting you, as I decided to stop engaging in an unproductive, ultimately no-win battle with EMAK. And when conflict is inevitable, you can often let your opponents play themselves out.

That's resilience. It's powerful to ignore people—to refuse to allow yourself to be affected by their anger or their hostility, to be above it all— because it shows confidence, and that's what Ali was doing: "Give me your best shot, George, if you're such a big, bad guy." I think that's a pretty powerful thing. But again, you have to *believe* it, or else it is not sustainable. You have to have faith in the course you have chosen.

That was never me. I always had to right every perceived wrong. And I lived that way until an internal transformation overtook me.

*   *   *

It's easy to become obsessed with control. Being in control of our lives gives us a sense of safety and security, but it is a false security.

Why do some people prefer to drive rather than fly? Statistically, flying is safer by several orders of magnitude—the fatality rate for commercial airline crashes is one in 11 million, versus one in 5,000 for car travelers. And yet, I know a number of people who will not fly. Maybe they had a bad turbulence experience once that scared them, or maybe the thought of being in the passenger seat, unable to take action if anything goes wrong, is viscerally frightening. *I don't know this pilot. What if he has a heart attack in the cockpit? For all I know, he's been drinking, or maybe he just isn't that skilled.*

But if I'm driving, I'm in control, so I'm going to drive seven hours to get from Nashville to Charlotte, North Carolina, instead of hopping on a one-hour flight. People make drives like that because they think the drive will be safer. It is *not* safer, of course, but because you are in control, you *feel* safer. *I'm a good driver, and I will be careful.* You drink coffee to stay awake, and you do your best to avoid the wackos on the road . . . but statistically, that is a very poor decision. And it's a decision some people make because of that false sense of control.

Getting back to my math analogy, the things that you imagine might happen to you if you decide to fly are *variables*—and if you're trying to control variables, then you have to look at why you have this need for control. I think human beings have a tendency to make themselves feel safe by compulsively overcontrolling their environments. But doing so gives a false sense of security, because you cannot control every variable—you can't even predict what variables might introduce themselves. So those people are just chasing safety . . . and to what end? Calvin Coolidge had it right when he said, *"If you see ten troubles coming down the road, you can be sure that nine will run into the ditch before they reach you."* [15]

You can even extend this risk-aversion paradigm to investing. If you think you are being ultrasafe by putting your cash under your mattress, you're kidding yourself. You might feel safer with your hidden cash stash because you know it can't be lost if the bank goes under . . . but that doesn't mean somebody can't simply steal it from your house.

Of course, most people aren't so paranoid that they won't put their money in the bank. But more realistically, you might feel safer if you put it in a low-interest savings account because you don't trust the stock market. ("It goes up and down, and that's scary. I don't like roller coasters!") That's still not a safe place for your money in the long run, though, because of inflation and the need to keep up. In fact, it's actually *unsafe* because you are going to lose purchasing power over time, and most savings accounts don't earn any meaningful interest. (And whatever interest you do earn is fully taxable.)

If you are a normal person, you will need to retire someday, which means you need to grow your nest egg. But after taxes and inflation, you are actually *losing* purchasing power if you keep your money in a savings account, almost as badly as you would if you kept it under your mattress. So even though the stock market can—and *will*—be volatile, and there are going to be years when you go, "Yikes! My net worth is down 20 percent!" it is still statistically far smarter in the long term to put your money in a diversified stock index fund.

*　*　*

Former Israeli Prime Minister Shimon Peres is said to have said, "If a problem has no solution it is not a problem, but a fact, not to be 'solved' but to be coped with over time."[16]

If you don't waste time fighting what you can't control, your blood pressure stays a lot lower. Accept and embrace the obstacles you face, and then do what you can to address and mitigate them. You have to say to yourself, *Okay, this is the reality: my wife is going to leave me, and my kid wants to disown me*; or *my best friend just slept with my fiancé, and I'm about to lose my job*; or *I was just diagnosed with a serious medical condition.* All of these things are just part of the human condition—and if you live long enough, some of them will happen to you. Accepting and embracing them doesn't mean being happy about your misfortune or not being frustrated; it just means being pragmatic, and saying, *This happened, and there has to be a reason why. It is part of the universe's plan. It is just the way life is sometimes. I need to embrace this reality and go forward with a plan to address this situation.*

I will give you an example from my own life. One of our current clients is a tech company I won't name. We're working on the marketing strategy for their AI, and it is at times exhilarating and at other times frustrating. This client is understandably highly alert to their competitors' every move, and that's making it challenging for us to market their premium structure—i.e., what you have to pay a subscription fee for versus what they offer for free. And because the competitive landscape keeps shifting, they keep having to reassess their strategy.

This periodic strategy reassessment can sometimes cause our work to have to suddenly pause mid-stream. We have six people dedicated to this client, and then suddenly they are "pencils down." That means six high-priced professionals are not fully utilized for a week or more, and we, of course, have to pay them until the client gives the go-ahead to restart the work.

It's certainly frustrating, but there's nothing we can do. Our client has to operate this way in such a fast-moving, competitive environment. We could resign from this client; we could tell them we can't operate this way. We could leave them and try to work for one of their competitors in the hope that these stops and starts wouldn't happen . . . but the competitors would almost certainly not be better, and very likely be worse. And there are a hundred agencies who would be thrilled to go to work for our current client and accept whatever terms they offer. I know the reality is that we are very fortunate to have such a prestigious client operating at the leading edge of technology.

So instead of being profitable the past two months, we posted a modest loss and are now not tracking to our budgeted profit target. But I don't panic. Sure, I'm worried, as digging out of a hole is always tough given the uncertain economic environment. But I don't lose sleep over it. I truly don't.

I *would* lose sleep if we had screwed up in some way—say, if we'd paid some high-priced people and they did lousy work, or if I found that we weren't attentive enough to the client's needs. But I could *control* that. I could fire those people.

But that is not the case. We haven't screwed up in any meaningful way, and we have earned a demanding client's trust over multiple years. The client is who they are, and they operate in an intensely competitive environment; we can't change this. And they always treat us with respect, thank us when we perform well, pay us fairly, and pay us on time. These are the hallmarks of a great client to have.

So I don't drive myself crazy trying to magically wishcast the client into being something they're not. I just do what I can to manage the situation and let the universe handle the rest—and am at peace with that.

* * *

It's tempting to catastrophize when you're faced with a difficult problem. That was me for most of my life. And part of me—the child part of me—still does that. That urge used to dominate my thinking. It doesn't anymore. In recent years, a kind of metamorphosis has happened to me. I don't know how; it just happened, like a switch finally got thrown in my brain. There is a certain serenity in just accepting what *is*. I can throw up my hands and face adversity with serenity as long as I didn't do something I shouldn't have done, or fail to handle something within my control—and even then I'm philosophical.

How did I achieve this equanimity? It's hard to say how the change came about—it can be difficult sometimes to read one's own mind. But I think it was during the years when I was mired in EMAK litigation while my marriage was experiencing significant turmoil. You win a seemingly major victory in the courtroom, and then they appeal and a higher court overrules that victory. Most notably, I won a critical case in the Delaware Court of Chancery, only to be reversed in part by the Delaware Supreme Court. (My lawyers and I actively considered appealing to the US Supreme Court, but I ultimately decided not to, given the time and cost that would have involved.) Through it all, I was writing checks and not advancing my life, and my career was being hindered by the enormous time and opportunity cost of these legal battles.

I fought these battles harder than I probably should have, driven by some noble but misguided desire to right an injustice I felt had been done to me. But I eventually realized I couldn't control what happens in court. If these guys using EMAK's corporate funds wanted to keep filing new motions and dispute every ruling that went in my favor, they had virtually unlimited money to do that with. It made me weary, trying to fight one pointless battle after the other when most of the other people affected by the situation had moved on.

I knew I had to change the game, or I was going to be bankrupt on top of being divorced. And of course, there was also the question of my health—you know what stress does to you. It was a very unpleasant way to live, and it wasn't going to work.

On the other side of this conflict was the billionaire EMAK investor who had ultimately gotten me fired . . . and in my opinion he was really good at this kind of thing. I felt strongly that, unlike me, he had no emotional stake in this fight—and I also felt strongly that he was not going to let me win, period.

I spent quite a bit of time in Delaware Court of Chancery, and one day, I just dropped everything. I decided, *I can't do this anymore.* I had to accept the reality that I was not going to win this litigation in the long run, and that I was not going to regain control of the company.

It was heading to bankruptcy anyway, which made the whole war even more pointless. I ended up fighting with the company in bankruptcy court, which is the stupidest thing you can do, because all your litigation against the company is frozen while the bankruptcy is being worked out. You can't sue a bankrupt company . . . but they are allowed to sue *you*, because that is a way for them to get money to pay their creditors. So even if I'd ultimately won, all my litigation against the company—and I *had* won a bunch of legal battles prior to the bankruptcy—would have been worthless.

So I had to settle. I got on a plane and went to meet the EMAK investor in Washington, DC. I didn't want to do it over the phone or via email. And I was fortunate that he even agreed to meet with me. If he were a jerk, he could have just said, "Screw you; speak to my lawyer." But he met with me, and we had a cordial conversation, the gist of which was, *Stop suing me and I will stop suing you.*

"Don," he said to me, "you're a good guy, but you can't win this game. Why are you doing this? You can't out-litigate the company, because you are fighting with scarce resources and don't know how to play this game. And with civil litigation, there's always another lawsuit, another appeal."

As that cliché from *The Godfather* goes, it was just business. I had formed the strong opinion that this guy is an expert at this game and he was approaching it objectively, without emotion, unlike me. "Sure," he said, "I'll drop our lawsuit."

I made that move as much from desperation as from strength, but it was still the right thing to do, because then I could move on. And that was cathartic. Suddenly, I wasn't waking up every day looking at legal briefs, and I could turn my focus to the question of how I was going to start building my net worth again.

But I couldn't just do it intellectually; I had to *feel* it. Intellectually, I knew this was a never-ending game I couldn't win because I didn't have enough resources, but I had to *know*, deep in my bones, that that was the right thing to do. And somehow, I converted to feeling it. Instead of doubling down like I would normally do ("Just work harder!"), I decided to change this game so that bad things could end up being good things.

* * *

A song from the 1979 film, *Monty Python's Life of Brian,* admonishes us to "always look on the bright side of life." That's good advice. That's how you cultivate resilience. You can't just wish a negative event out of your life . . . because it *happened*. Muhammad Ali couldn't pretend he wasn't taking those punches, and when life punches *you* in the face, there's no celestial, existential litigation to make it *un*happen.

Difficulties in your life need to be faced, but they can't be allowed to destroy your confidence.

And if they haven't happened, no amount of planning and fretting is going to guarantee that they *won't* happen. But as long as you are behaving well, as long as you are acting with integrity and doing your part, those negative events are not unendurable.

When I finally took that attitude onboard, I became philosophical: This is God's plan for me, and somehow this is what is supposed to happen, and things will end up better in the long run. Maybe I'll ultimately be thankful that my career-ending knee injuries led me to the once-in-a-lifetime experience of Studio 54 and the insane world of disco. Maybe when that client fires me, I'll find a new client with whom I can have a more productive, more profitable relationship. Maybe the end of my marriage will lead to finding my true soulmate. Whatever it is, every setback or loss presents an opportunity to be more accepting of what looks like a bad break.

It's difficult to say all this without resorting to some terribly overused cliché about making lemonade out of lemons, or how when one door closes, another one opens. But that's what can always happen—if you let it. Some people who become disabled later claim that their life changed for the better. Maybe losing their sight caused their remaining senses to engage with their surroundings in ways they never could have imagined. Maybe losing the ability to walk motivated them to learn a musical instrument or to earn a PhD in Renaissance literature. Or maybe it just helped them clarify their values and appreciate what was really important to them. Initially they were depressed, but a year later they had become philosophical about their loss, and they were grateful for what they had—so they were actually happier than they had been.

On the other hand, there have been studies of lottery winners, and a year after winning, many of them were less happy because they had to move out of their community or greedy relatives started coming out of the woodwork. And, of course, some of them went bankrupt because they didn't know how to handle the money—and they were worse off.

It is mind-blowing to imagine that if you want to be happy a year from now, statistically you may be better off losing a limb than winning the lottery. But that is sometimes the case.

I don't know what this says about me psychologically, but I am more at peace when I hear bad news than I am when everything is going well. (I guess that is called "being Jewish.") I don't *want* bad things, but I have a certain fatalistic calmness about them. When everything is going well, I have anxiety. It's just how my body reacts—my gut. We Jews have a tradition of saying *kinehora* when we catch ourselves thinking or talking about how well things are going; it's a Yiddish word that translates roughly as "no evil eye," and it means, essentially, "knock on wood." And to fail to say *kinehora* is to invite fate to turn your good luck to bad.

Kinehora may seem like a silly superstition, but knocking on wood is sometimes all you *can* do. How do you prepare yourself for a hundred-year flood? Well, one way is not to worry about it, because you can't control it. You can do your best to prepare for the proverbial rainy day. Make sure you have a nest egg, and maybe don't buy a house right on a fault line in an earthquake zone, or in a fire-prone area, or right on the beach in a storm-prone area. Buy insurance for disasters, including life insurance if you have a family. Do whatever you can reasonably do to mitigate the consequences of bad luck.

But spending too much time trying to manage risk—which is the same thing as trying to control all the variables—is just not productive. You can't succeed, because you *can't* control all the variables. It's a rigged game of whack-a-mole. There's always a new variable that surfaces, and you just have to accept that there is always risk that you can't anticipate or hedge against. And if you try, you will spend your life fighting off demons and not growing and not living. I think a lot of people do that. The fear of the unknown is too great, versus accepting the unknown as a potential great thing. There's a lot of upside to any situation, if you're willing to look for it.

Moreover, it's important to remember that our inability to predict the future cuts both ways—just as we can't predict when bad luck will ambush us out of the blue, we can't predict when it will miraculously spare us. That's the meaning of the Calvin Coolidge quotation that I referenced earlier in this chapter: not every looming catastrophe actually comes to pass.

You have to be observant instead of trying to be preemptive, to react to what actually happens as opposed to what *might* happen. Keep an eye on all the moving parts of your life, and just be aware, so you can see when something goes wrong—and then react as quickly as you can. We have a list of five variables that indicate the health of Omelet. For example, one of them is the sales pipeline: How many opportunities do we have? How big are they? What's the probability they are going to convert? What's the net expected value of the pipeline (size of opportunity multiplied by the probability of winning the business)? What are our receivables? Are some clients not paying, or paying sixty days later than they are supposed to? Monitor the metrics of your company's health, and you'll get an early indicator that you'd better do something about an emergent problem. Being observant and not having your head in the sand, thinking you are controlling everything, is really important if you want to avoid being blindsided.

But at some point, you just have to let go, accept uncertainty, and even embrace it. Do your part, have your antennae up so you can see what's going on and deal with it . . . and more often than not, the cards will end up in your favor, as long as you're working hard and not refusing to acknowledge reality.

*　*　*

I'm under a considerable amount of stress right now as I draft this chapter. I have business challenges I won't get into here, but they are considerable. I recently concluded negotiations to settle all my divorce obligations with my ex-wife. I am getting married again, which is wonderful, but requires a lot of time to prepare for.

Also, I had major spine surgery a year ago, and am still doing extensive physical therapy. *And* I'm writing this book.

A sane person *should* be really stressed out. And I'm not saying I'm walking around whistling. There are nights when my eyes pop open at 3 a.m. But by and large, I am relatively peaceful. I shouldn't be, rationally speaking, but I am . . . and I have to admit that I don't know *exactly* why.

Maybe it's because I chose most of these paths. My business problems may be vexing, but I could have chosen a career as a dance instructor, couldn't I?

My divorce settlement may be . . . well, let's just say it's more than I would have hoped for. But nobody made me do that. I could have gone to court and perhaps done better, but the only guarantee there would be that more money would be expended on legal fees and more time burned. And my second wedding may have been time-consuming to prepare for—but in both cases, I chose my path.

Nobody told me I had to write this book right now. In theory, it would have been easier not to start the book in the middle of planning a wedding and recovering from surgery. But I made that decision, and it's one I wouldn't take back, because I really wanted to get this book done and done well.

I take comfort in having made all of those choices. In each case, I could have said no, but I made that decision, so I don't second-guess it. I've come to terms with my choices so that I'm comfortable with them—including my bad choices.

I think it's just the accumulation of life experiences that brought me to this place of acceptance. When you are old enough to have made certain mistakes multiple times, you come to realize that it is futile to fight reality, and futile to keep second-guessing yourself. And it's *really* futile to blame other people for your own errors.

I don't think there's a formula for creating this peace of mind: "Do these eight things and take vitamin C and you'll get this way." I guess I just got pummeled in the ring of life enough, and then I flipped the game over. I changed the game from fighting reality to accepting and embracing it. And that certainly doesn't mean being happy with *all* of reality. But just not fighting it took an enormous weight off of me. I also saw that sometimes, bad things that happen lead to good things, so why fight them?

I do everything I can do, and then whatever happens just *happens*. The chips will fall where they may, and I will do my best to maximize the next round of chips.

Intellectually, I probably knew all of this thirty years ago. But you have to internalize it. You can't just say, "Yeah, I'm going to achieve perfect Zen," and then somebody cuts you off on the highway and you flip out and try to chase them down. You can't intellectually buy this new *que será, será* outlook and then not change your behavior.

My goal for this book is for you not to have to endure decades of internal turmoil, litigation, and constant battle. I can speak knowledge- ably about this because I suffered from not doing it. I've made a conscious effort to modify my own behavior. My emotional algorithm changed in the same way Google's search algorithm changes when they need to update it, and new things popped up. And I realized, *Ah, this game is so much easier and more pleasant and more productive.* My mother, may she rest in peace, always said, "Donny always needs to learn everything the hard way." She was right.

I don't take bad luck personally anymore; I just remind myself that *of course this is the way it is—this is the way it has got to be. And things will somehow end up better because of it.*

CHAPTER TWELVE

Don't Fight the Tape:
When to Let Go of Your Sunk Costs

THERE'S AN OLD EXPRESSION ON WALL STREET: "DON'T FIGHT the tape." It dates back to an era when stock prices were printed on a ticker tape, and it means, "Don't make a trade that goes against the prevailing market trends."[17] That ticker tape reflected hard reality, and only a gambler or a fool would bet against reality.

That expression is still used today in the investment world, but it can be applied to other areas of concern as well—a struggling business, for example, or even a marriage or other personal relationship.

Not fighting the tape means acknowledging that the direction you're headed in is the wrong one. It could be a stock you're holding on to, it could be a relationship, it could be business, it could be friendship—whatever it is, it's going the wrong way, and rather than fighting that understanding, you have to accept it.

Unfortunately, too many people try to fight the tape because they find the alternative—accepting a loss—too unpleasant.

But you can't escape the unpleasantness; one way or another, the inevitability of the tape is going to catch up with you. My dentist used to send a little postcard reminder to schedule a cleaning, and the front of the postcard read, "Are your teeth bothering you? Just ignore them, and they will go away!" The same can be said about the problems with a failing business or marriage, or the downward trajectory of a long-held stock.

As the auto mechanic says in a Fram oil filter commercial from the early '70s,[18] "You can pay me now . . . or you can pay me later"—i.e., buy a $4 oil filter now, or pay for a $200 bearing job later. (Respectively $35 and $1,552 in 2025 dollars.) You don't change your oil because you don't want to take the time, and because the job is dirty and unpleasant . . . and then, all of a sudden, your whole engine is messed up.

If you try to ignore the unpleasantness in your life and hope it will go away, you're in for a rude surprise, because it doesn't. If you ignore a problem, it is only going to fester. It may very well fester into an ulcer and manifest as anger directed at people who don't deserve it. It will eventually cause other health problems as well, and your blood pressure will go up.

*　*　*

In this chapter, I'll be applying the phrase, "Don't fight the tape" to other areas of life—relationships and business enterprises, litigation, et cetera— but since the phrase originated in the stock market, let's start there.

Many of us have emotional ties to the stocks we pick—that is, to the businesses we invest in. You've seen horse-racing fans get pretty worked up at the track, right? Emotionally, it's a lot like that. (And yes, I'll be discussing gambling later in the chapter.)

In the old days, when you'd pick your own stocks and not just throw your money into a mutual fund, you did your research. "Wow, IBM is the greatest company," you'd think, and you'd buy as many shares as you could afford—the same way a racing fan might place a big bet on a horse he likes.

But then the stock doesn't go anywhere—the market is up, but IBM isn't going up with it. And then two years go by and you still haven't sold it, and now there is an opportunity cost: you could have taken your money out of IBM and invested in a more successful company, or at least put it into an index fund that would have kept up with the overall performance of the market.

But you don't want to acknowledge that you were wrong.

Sometimes there are technical reasons why stocks underperform, like a bad trading pattern. When that happens, the smart traders—who have no emotional attachment to their investments—will sell it because it didn't meet their expectations within a defined period of time.

* * *

Most people don't acknowledge when something they're attached to is going the wrong way. They hold stocks that aren't doing well, as we've been discussing, but they also stay in relationships way too long, or they refuse to fire an employee who is clearly out of his or her depth. And the reason, sadly, is often kindness. In the case of a bad relationship, the couple are both nice people and neither wants to hurt the other's feelings, and so a year goes by . . . and another year, and another. If you're doing that, you're fighting the tape. The relationship is going in the other direction. Acknowledge it, embrace it, and then pivot.

Knowing when to pivot is really an art, not a science. With stocks, it can be that you define a specific goal and trading pattern, and if that stock doesn't meet expectations, you have to get rid of it. But for most things in life, it is not that black and white. It is the failed business model you don't want to acknowledge is wrong: we just need *one* more client, or we just need to move to this location or change our strategy a little bit, versus saying, "You know what? This thing is done. Don't throw good money after bad."

At some point you have to acknowledge failure, and only with hindsight can you be positive when that is (or was). Even the best judgement you can bring to bear is just an assessment of probabilities, because it is never 100 percent certain that you will succeed or fail. You *might* get a new client—you can always get lucky—but that doesn't mean that you still shouldn't exit the business. So you're just weighing your options, toggling the probabilities: *Can I get into something new? Should I take my money out while I still can? Should I close the company down and give people severance while I still can versus continuing to pour money into it? Should I sell the company for a price I find underwhelming?*

You have to have the objectivity to be able to look at those questions, particularly when you are an entrepreneur, because there is writing on the wall all the time: are we going to get undercut by new competitors with fresher ideas? You are constantly assessing—because you *need* to be.

On the other hand, as an entrepreneur, you have to be optimistic in the long term. You have to be *eternally* optimistic, or you will die every day. But there is always some gremlin lurking that can take you down, and that optimism can't blind you, so you also have to be brutally honest in the short term. You have to be eternally optimistic in the long term, but in the meantime, you have to be honest: if you are burning cash, are you going to keep these five underperforming employees on longer than you should?

It is the same way with litigation; if a long, grinding courtroom battle begins to go badly for you, then you have to ask yourself, "Should I fold my cards and settle?"

As I described in the previous chapter, I finally gave up on my litigation against EMAK. I realized I was going to lose, and that I was *already* losing, and that even if I won in court, I would keep losing because my pockets weren't deep enough to fund a defense of my victory against what seemed to me to be EMAK's inevitable endless appeals.

You have to have self-awareness and be as dispassionate as possible about your prospects for victory, because it is just false ego to push something longer than it should be pushed.

* * *

I was smart enough not to try to fight the tape when the time came for me to exit the lacrosse team in my senior year. I instinctively cut my losses.

My knee was a big problem, of course. I'd lost half a step, and in my game that could be everything. But the bigger issue was that I'd taken a little time for introspection, and I realized, *I am just not that into it anymore,*

*and the trend isn't good . . . and I'm going to end up riding the bench if I
don't get my head out of my ass.*

I remember looking around at my teammates. We had recruited a
really top-shelf freshman class, and all these guys were just like I'd been as
a freshman: this was their dream. They trained year-round, and they were
passionate. We had also brought in two future first-team All-American
midfielders via transfer from the Naval Academy and Washington and
Lee. I, on the other hand, felt like I'd "been there, done that," as they
say. I'd already won a national championship, so what was left for me to
accomplish in this sport? (That freshman class and key transfers formed
the nucleus of Hopkins teams that won three national championships in a
row—1978, 1979, and 1980. Only one other team—Princeton University
between 1996 and 1998—accomplished this three-peat since the NCAA
playoff era began in 1971.)

These guys all loved practicing; I dreaded going to practice in 1977.
And that was a problem for me as a player. I couldn't just use brute
strength to carry the day; as I've said, I'm a relatively little guy for a contact
sport like lacrosse at the top-tier, and if I'm not passionate and out-hustling people, I don't have any role in the game at that level. In my prime
with two good wheels, I could compete with anyone at any level, because I
was quicker and tougher. But when you lose your edge and you don't have
that drive anymore, it's all over for you as a top-shelf athlete—and I was
smart enough to realize that. I didn't try to hang onto an athletic career
that clearly was circling the drain.

So I pivoted to become the best, coolest dancer I could be, rather than
a mediocre lacrosse player. I'm sure I'm still the only player in the 142-year
history of Johns Hopkins lacrosse who has ever left the team to become a
dance instructor—and I may be the first in the history of the sport.

In hindsight, it's amazing that I was able to do that so quickly, after
having been a top player for all those years, and given that my whole life
and my whole identity were wrapped up in the game. I'm not sure how
quickly I would be able to do something like that now.

*   *   *

There are three main reasons most people try to fight the tape rather than accept a loss: sunk costs, odds delusion, and selective perception.

First, let's look at what logicians call the *sunk-cost fallacy*. In economic theory, a sunk cost is money, time, or effort you've *already* expended—which is irrelevant to any decision you need to make today and going forward. And those costs are considered "sunk" because they are *gone*. You can't get that time back, just as you can't get back that slim figure you had when you were younger. The money you've invested—let's say you used your savings to start this business—is gone.

Now, that doesn't necessarily mean you should quit the business if it's struggling; you just have to evaluate your options without the emotional weight of *I've already put so much into it*. Whatever you've already invested is still irrelevant in terms of what you invest going forward.

Obviously, a business isn't the only thing that can have sunk costs: "Oh my God, my marriage! I have three kids, but this marriage is over. I know it. We don't have sex; I think she is having an affair. Every time she talks, I cringe. I don't want to be married to her anymore . . . but oh my God, I can't afford a divorce. What are the kids going to do? All of our friends are mutual friends, and what are we going to do about *that*? I can't afford to move out of the house. We just . . ."

You get the picture, I'm sure, especially if you or someone you know has fallen down that particular rabbit hole. The kids, the house, the mutual friends, the years you've both put into the marriage already—all of those things are sunk costs. And because they're sunk, it's hard to let go of them. I get it.

But a marriage doesn't repair itself, and when it eventually unravels all the way, it will end just like not firing poor Tom ended for our hypothetical business owner in Chapter 5. Like it or not, you will *have* to fire him eventually, or someday he will leave on his own—disgruntled, without notice—and you would have been far better off proactively addressing the problem. You don't want to send people to the unemployment line, but if the business can't support itself, you'll just end up closing it and not paying severance because you waited too long. If a small business has twenty employees and five of them don't pull their weight, if you don't get rid of those five—as hard as that is—then the other fifteen are going to lose their jobs, too, because there won't be a company. It is therefore not kind to keep those five people on.

Likewise, it is not an act of kindness to stay married to someone you don't love anymore, just to spare them (and yourself) the shock of a divorce. Now, if you just can't do this to your kids, then you might accept that you are going to be miserable for their sake. You might make a decision to stay in your unhappy marriage—but that's not the same thing as fighting the tape and pretending your marriage is working. You are doing it with open eyes. You can be conscious of what that decision means and say, "I *choose* to be miserable, because I'm not going to do this to my kids." You will still be unhappy, but at least you are not kidding yourself.

The sunk-cost fallacy is what prevents many people from addressing problems, whether in business or relationships. For whatever reason, they want to paint red flags green rather than dealing with them: "I've already put $5 million into this company! I refused an acquisition offer three years ago, and if I hadn't done that I could have gotten out with a really nice gain. But now I've doubled down on that investment and I've got all these sunk costs."

Sunk-cost attachment is a powerful human emotion. People would be a lot happier and businesses would be a lot more successful if we could all just learn to cut our losses and get out when the time comes. But it is very difficult for humans to do that. You think that if you hang onto this failing marriage or that failing business, you're somehow protecting your investment: "I've held this stock for two years, and I just want to break even."

"I've put ten years into this marriage. I was in my prime when I got married, and I looked the best I'll ever look, and now I'm older and we have kids, and I've invested all this time. We've got to find a way to make it work."

It doesn't work—or at least, it very rarely does. All you are doing is doubling down on a bad bet. The right way to address sunk costs is to evaluate them from today going forward. In all probability, you have *already* lost the money you invested. You've *already* invested your time in that marriage. You cannot let that past investment factor into your decision *today*. You therefore have to evaluate the value of the thing *today*: "Would I marry this person again today?" is the right question to ask. Would I invest in this business today? Would I buy this stock today at this price? Those are the questions that should guide your decisions.

And emotionally, it's not easy to do that. I don't know if it is the way humans are wired, but we have a hard time evaluating these things rationally—and I'm no different. I'm not saying I'm perfect at any of this. Far from it.

*   *   *

That's the tricky thing. You have to be able to weigh risks and anticipate future consequences—but the picture is generally not black and white. There's always a chance the marriage will turn around, or the business will turn around. Sometimes it is a 0.01 percent chance . . . but sometimes it is 20 percent. What kind of odds justify sticking it out? Obviously, if you knew your chances of saving your marriage or your business were only 0.01 percent, you'd throw in the towel—but how do you evaluate risk/reward when your odds are 20 or 30 percent? Those odds aren't good . . . but they're good enough to inspire hope, aren't they?

The problem is that your hope is going to get you killed. And that's really the problem—that tension between necessary optimism and necessary realism. We have to be hopeful, or we are going to kill ourselves. But at the same time, your hope is going to get you killed if it keeps you from addressing the problem. As I said, the tricky thing is that it's rarely 100 percent obvious that whatever bad bet you've made is a *doomed* bet, and the casino already has your money.

We humans tend to get delusional about odds. We never think our chance of success is one in a million. For example, I once had to attend traffic school after getting a speeding ticket, and there was a video about how important it is to wear your seatbelt. Afterward, during class discussion, one guy raised his hand and said, "I will never wear a seatbelt. I was in an accident once, in a convertible, and I wasn't wearing my seatbelt, and I got thrown from my car—and the car blew up ten seconds later. If I'd been wearing a seatbelt, I'd be dead now, so don't tell me it is safer."

Of course, most of us understand that that's a one-in-a-million outcome. But the point of this example is that there's always someone who can say, "If I followed your advice, I would be dead." There are over eight billion human beings on Earth, collectively making billions of decisions every moment, and it would be shocking if a one-in-a-million freak occurrence *didn't* happen to everyone from time to time. If you're having marital problems, one friend might tell you to divorce your wife, and then another friend might say, "Not so fast . . . *my* wife hit the lottery the day I got divorced." The odds against your wife winning the lottery may be astronomical, but if you're human, you'll at least be a bit tempted to listen to friend #2.

A friend of mine recently told me a story about a client who won a lot of money in the lottery, and my friend said to him, "I'm excited for you. I'm very glad you bought the ticket. But even though you won, I would still have to advise you that, statistically, you shouldn't have bought it."

People think this way about investments all the time: No matter how obviously toxic a stock may be, no matter how much smart money is selling it, there's always someone who thinks, "Oh my God, GE is going down . . . so let me get it while I can, because it's bound to bounce back!" That brings to mind another Wall Street expression: "Don't try to catch a falling knife."

You can see how this compounds with the sunk-cost fallacy. You make a rash business decision, or you marry someone you've just started dating, or you buy a stock you think is undervalued, all because you're so invested in believing that the odds are much better than they are. Then, when it starts going badly, you've already got ten years together plus kids as a factor in the marriage, a business that you've labored at and put every penny of your savings into, or the lost value of the initial stock investment. Those sunk costs, plus the indignity of having to admit you were wrong, cause you to overestimate the chances that things will get better—and you double down.

But you can't fight the tape. Even if you are the one-in-a-million guy who survives a car crash because you didn't wear your seatbelt, that's not a smart way to play the game of life.

Gambling, of course, is another area where people ignore sunk costs—it's a sunk-cost *and* odds-delusion issue. You go to Las Vegas and you tell everyone, "Okay, I'm going to gamble $200, and if I lose it, I get up and walk away."

But you don't walk away. When the moment comes, you think, "I can't keep losing forever!" Besides, you want to break even. And then maybe you *do* get back to even—but now you're winning, and breaking even is no longer the goal. You want to feel like a *winner*. So you keep playing, and you lose all your winnings, and now you're even deeper in the hole than you were before.

It's just human nature. When our odds of winning are 10–90, we still think they are 50–50, or even 90–10, because otherwise, nobody would ever buy a lottery ticket.

Finally, there's the problem of selective perception. For example, when you ask someone for an honest critique of your work, your clothes, your looks, or anything else you take pride in, you selectively hear what you want to hear. If your wife says, "It's a shame you've let yourself get so out of shape, since you're so handsome," you may only hear, "You're so handsome!"

Most of us consume mass media in the same way. You listen selectively to the news, and you listen specifically for information that is going to reinforce whatever you already believe—because changing your mind can be uncomfortable and therefore unpleasant.

The same goes for a business or a relationship you want to save. You will interpret data in the most positive way . . . and you are just kidding yourself. You will endure any amount of cognitive dissonance in order to avoid accepting data that goes against what you want to be true.

* * *

Let me give you a hypothetical illustrating all these factors in action: Let's say there's a woman, forty years old, never been married, and wants kids very badly. She's a career woman who delayed marriage, and now she appears very unsatisfied.

She is with a guy who is once or twice divorced. They live together, and at one point, they schedule their wedding . . . and then they call it off a week beforehand. Let's assume the guy is thinking, *I just don't know if I want to get married again.*

She moved to another state to be with him. She left a well-paying job behind. After the wedding was called off, she told everyone that they were still getting married, and that this was just a little delay. It is clear to any objective observer she should just leave him already. She needs to move on, or she is not going to get married to anyone, ever. This guy is not going to get married again; he has already got a kid, he is in his forties, and he just wants to have a little fun. But she wants to be married with a family—and the clock is ticking for her.

Sure, there is always the hope that this guy will come around. Maybe they *will* get married and live happily ever after. He probably tells her that because he doesn't want to be unkind, although he may be out looking for another girl as we speak. That's what a lot of guys do when they are looking for something "better." That is just the hard reality. A lot of guys can be comfortable for a long time with just a physical relationship. He doesn't care if the woman is deluding herself—because *he* doesn't have a clock.

And the hypothetical woman in this story knows all this, but she doesn't want to face it. She needs to move on with her life because she will be forty-one soon, and then forty-two. The days go slowly, but the years go fast.

Maybe the worst part is that she's *letting* him do this. It's not his fault, assuming he doesn't lie to her and say, "Yeah, honey, I'll be ready in another six months." And why is she letting him get away with this? Because she's in the grip of all three of the delusions I've described in this chapter:

Sunk costs: She's been with this guy for a long time—she even moved out of state to be with him—and at her age, the prospect of admitting to herself that it was all for nothing has to be pretty daunting.

Selective perception—especially selective hearing: She discounts it and forgets about it when he says he's not sure whether he wants another lifetime commitment. But every time he says, "I love you," she hears *that!*

Odds delusion: There is always a chance that maybe he will come around and they will get married. You just have to do the expected value calculation: what is the probability of that, given the data? It's likely around 10 percent. The number of couples like these two who live happily ever after is vanishingly small—but she can't see that. She'll keep holding out hope, believing her odds of marrying him are far higher than they really are.

*   *   *

Now, she *could* decide to be happy with that: "You know what, I don't care if I'm ever married. I accept that kids may not be in my future. I'm going to enjoy this relationship for what it is, and I'm going to look for somebody else as well, just like he's doing, and I'm fine with it." (I know plenty of successful women who feel exactly this way—and good for them.)

But that's not the way some people think.

*   *   *

This is a critical thing to know in life—how not to stay too long at the fair. So how *do* you know? What are the signs? What is it that you shouldn't be ignoring?

Your gut knows. Your gut knows that you lost your top employee because she saw the writing on the wall or you couldn't pay her enough. Your gut knows that you are losing more pitches than you are winning. Your gut knows that your wife is having an affair—or at least it knows when she can no longer stand the sound of your laugh.

Your gut knows whether your personal passion as an entrepreneur is diminished, because you are not getting up extra early to get to the office extra early. You are just going through the motions, and you're looking at your numbers through rose-colored glasses. The signs are there.

As an entrepreneur, it is hard to acknowledge when your baby is failing. And maybe you could pull it out. But there's a point where the risk/

return potential goes south. You see that it is taking longer to collect your receivables, and your cash flow is getting stretched out. And yes, there is a 10 percent chance that you've left a lot of money on the table, but you have to go with the odds. Ask yourself, "What did I learn, and what could I pivot to?" Because otherwise, you can just keep pouring money into that company . . . and all of a sudden you are bankrupt.

If you are an entrepreneur, the best thing is to have a dashboard with early warning signs on it, which generally will relate to cash position and cash flow, your burn rate versus your collection rate, et cetera. But there is data . . . and then there is your gut. In the end, it is a matter of reading the tea leaves.

And relationships are the same way. You know when, to quote the title of a 2009 romantic comedy, *He's Just Not That Into You*. Now, when is that point? When are differences irreconcilable? There's no hard rule for measuring that, but it tends to be pretty clear if you let your gut talk to you. You know when things are not working out, because you can pick up on the clues: she is not returning your texts as fast as she used to, she is not putting your picture on her social media accounts, or she is going out with her friends a lot more than she used to. The signs are all there—you just have to realize it. You can't fight the tape, and the tape says she is just not that into you. You cannot turn that around. You can't fight the tape with kindness or flowers.

It is not that some people have crystal balls and can see the future and some don't. It's just that some people pay attention to what they already know . . . and some don't.

*   *   *

Now let's paint a picture of what happens if you bite the bullet and deal in reality: stop ignoring warning signs, cut him or her loose, or close down the company. What's the upside that awaits if you are willing to go through that temporary pain?

Well, a couple of things. One, you are being honest with yourself, and there is a certain level of comfort and self-respect that comes with that.

You are making a hard decision, and you know some people are going to second-guess it and maybe even hate you for it—for example, if you close a business, or if you say goodbye to a loving wife because you just aren't into her anymore. But you are making a tough decision, and you are doing it not because you're a jerk or because you're a liar or a cheat; you are doing it because it is the right thing to do, and you can take comfort in that.

Secondly, a more practical consideration is that you live to fight another day. If you leave your marriage, and do it with compassion and dignity, you can move on with your life and hopefully find your true soulmate (and so can your spouse). Even if you don't find that ultimate love, you won't be living a lie, and you will be ready for new horizons.

And again, there are probabilities to be calculated. Because maybe there is an 18 percent chance that you can turn that company around, or that your marriage will turn around. That's not an insignificant chance . . . but it's not a good one either.

We are good at kidding ourselves because facing reality is painful. It is going to require action. You are going to have to move. At some point, you just have to concede that you can't fight the tape, acknowledge reality, cut your losses, and get out. It takes a lot of courage, but when it's done, there is a certain freedom. I stopped that litigation with EMAK—even though if I had kept fighting and won, I could have potentially recouped tens of millions of dollars—because I could see that my odds of winning were growing slimmer by the day. I had a lot of sunk costs . . . but I also still had a lot more to lose.

When I gave up on that battle, it was a weight lifted off my shoulders because I had finally faced reality. Then I pivoted, and Omelet popped up.

And I wouldn't have been able to do that if I'd kept fighting that damn tape.

CHAPTER THIRTEEN

Fear of Failure—and How to Manage It

Failure is a paradox . . . or more to the point, *fear* of failure is a paradox. It's a fear that can paralyze us and discourage us from acting in the world—and yet it also motivates us to maximize our efforts. Properly managed, fear of failure can not only make us bold enough to do what needs to be done, but also restrain us from acting recklessly.

So there is a balance to be struck: We need not fear failure so much that we are intimidated by the task at hand—but enough to ensure that we *really* try our best to succeed.

Speaking of which, I hate this sentence: "At least I tried my best." I dislike not just the sentence itself, but also the underlying philosophy. The idea that it's no big deal to fail as long as you tried is a pernicious notion that has wormed its way into our culture—which is why, for example, we have things today like participation trophies in kids' sports, and it's why sometimes those games don't even have winners and losers.

"I tried my best. Everybody fails." I have no tolerance for that excuse. It invites responses like, "Well, your best stinks," or "If that's your best, maybe you're just not cut out for this." Success *matters*, and you've got to find a way. You may not be faster or bigger than the other guy, but you've

155

got to find a way to win—out-hustle him or outwork him. There are so many variables you can control. "I tried my best" is the ultimate cop-out, one that is often intended to halt any criticism, no matter how much it may be needed.

That said, failure will come, of course—we all fail sometimes. The occasional failure is the price we pay for trying and stretching our horizons. But if you've truly done everything you could, even that failure can lead to new doors opening. People will respect you for the genuine effort you've made.

And of course, there are always lessons to be learned from failure. Sometimes you give it your all—you do your part, you work your butt off, and you act ethically. You do all those things . . . and then the market turns against you, or it turns out that your business premises were false. Or maybe your marriage falls apart because you didn't marry the person you thought you did. Whenever you fail at anything, you have to trust that there will be lessons in that failure and take comfort in learning those lessons.

But you can't be seduced into thinking that your failure is no big deal—that it's something you can just shrug off. You still have to regard a failure *as a failure*. When we fail, we need to feel the bitter disappointment—and perhaps even a touch of shame—that motivates us *not* to fail next time.

"It's okay—I tried. It just didn't work out." That's like sitting on the couch expecting things will just magically work out for you someday, when it's your turn to have a good day. You proclaim, "God's got a plan and He'll take care of me!" But you're lazy and you're not doing anything to further that plan, if there is one.

That's not how the world works. You have to do your part. Failure will come when you're taking risks, and you have to be okay with that. But not to worry about it, or not to regret it when it happens, is a cop-out. It gives you permission to fail.

You can't fear failure *too* much, because then you'll never take risks. But one of the most reliable ways to succeed is to have a lot of self-imposed pressure. How did Ohio State win the 2024 national college football championship after losing to 20.5-point underdog and bitter rival Michigan in that incredible final regular season game upset?[19] They must have been incredibly demoralized. The coach was probably going to get fired if he didn't win the national championship. And, of course, there were the players' great expectations: once you graduate from college, you'll never have another opportunity to win that football championship.

So they felt a lot of pressure—and then they went on a run and whacked every team they played after that.

The lesson here is that you need to put a lot of pressure on yourself in order to succeed, but you can't allow that pressure to paralyze you. Fear of failure, if it is too intense, will probably enhance the probability of failure, so it's not productive. But not to fear failure at all is to invite it.

I'm an entrepreneur, so I don't fear failure—and I've had a couple of big failures in my life. (That EMAK litigation and subsequent bankruptcy comes to mind; so does the closure of my hedge fund in the aftermath of the 2008 financial crisis and Madoff fraud.) Would I rather not have had those? I certainly would be a lot wealthier now if I avoided those events. I'm not saying I'm a better person for those experiences, but I definitely learned a lot from them, both in business and in life.

Everything I've really wanted in my life, I went for it—hard. Everything I did, I gave it my all, in sports and dancing and business. I say this not to toot my own horn, but to highlight that I was able to achieve success beyond my natural abilities through hard work and determination, and that you can do the same.

*　*　*

Another phrase I dislike is *work-life balance*, which carries a suggestion that work is bad, and your life should be arranged to minimize the amount of work you need to do. That notion bugs me because, as an entrepreneur, there is no difference between my work and my life. They blend together, and that's not a burden to me. Why should there be a line separating those spheres? My work isn't separate from my life; it's *part* of my life. I socialize with people I do business with. I'm always thinking about work, and that's not a bad thing. If I'm successful at work, I can take great vacations and I can afford nice things. I also really enjoy work—the game of it, the camaraderie of working in teams, the highs of a big sale, the constant challenge of problems to solve.

I imagine if you're a blue-collar worker, then maybe you're not living your job and taking it home. But as an entrepreneur or an aspiring top-level corporate executive, there is no such thing as "work-life balance." You have to be living it, and you have to constantly be selling. Everyone you meet, you size up: *Is this a prospective client? Who might they know?* And this "always on" mentality must be fun and joyful, not a burden.

Work is contribution. It's not just what you get for yourself; it's what you get for other people. So, if you're allergic to work, you're not part of the social contract under which everybody's contributing to everybody else, doing their best and paying their taxes and creating value for other people. That's how society functions, and society disintegrates when that contract is not honored. That's why communism doesn't work; I don't believe that most people are inherently lazy, but if you give some people the chance, they will take the easy way out.

I think this attitude is a generational thing. Ironically, it's something that happens when societies become great and prosperous. Nations and empires from the Roman Empire onward have had this experience: A society becomes wealthy . . . and then it gets kind of flabby. It happened to Britain after World War I. The empire didn't fall overnight—they still had India and a lot of the Middle East—but they were declining noticeably.

Then again, how do you stay on top? Inevitably, you'll take your eye off the ball, and there'll be somebody hungrier or younger than you who works harder. Back in the 1960s and '70s, whenever somebody went to Japan or Korea, they noticed that the people there worked *all the time*—while Americans were now focused on the forty-hour work week and unions were demanding even more ways to make work less central to people's lives. "It's just a matter of time," some people predicted. "They're going to eat our lunch." But nobody listened.

It's the paradox of success (this chapter is full of paradoxes!): You've won the Super Bowl; now how do you keep your edge? How do you keep from getting complacent? When we succeed long enough and well enough, we begin to feel *entitled* to that success. But there's no entitlement to being the dominant nation on earth, or to being a wealthy, successful individual. You can only coast one way—downhill.

Sometimes, loss of passion contributes to the problem. I ran into that in lacrosse during my senior year at Hopkins, after sitting out my junior year with injuries. It was a combination of factors that sapped my drive to succeed: I'd discovered dancing, and my enthusiasm for the sport I loved was waning. And then I looked at all those gung-ho freshmen on the team—and they were just like me when I was a freshman: they were maniacally dedicated and focused (not to mention they were big and strong). And I thought, *I want to do the Hustle.* I was very talented—and fast—but without that extra little edge of passion, I was a sitting duck, destined to get ousted from the starting position I held. I preempted that inevitable crushing ego blow by leaving the team.

Andrew Grove, in his book, *Only the Paranoid Survive*, warns that you have to be constantly on the lookout. You've got to be paranoid, he says, and you've got to be looking ahead. "Business success contains the seeds of its own destruction," Grove writes. "The more successful you are, the more people want a chunk of your business and then another chunk and then another, until there is nothing."[20]

Grove also notes that "the most important role of managers is to create an environment in which people are passionately dedicated to winning in the marketplace. Fear plays a major role in creating and maintaining such passion. Fear of competition, fear of bankruptcy, fear of being wrong, and fear of losing can all be powerful motivators."[21]

You've got to work hard, and you've got to *keep* working hard even after you've succeeded. You can't rest on your laurels—individually, or as a company, a society, or a country. You can't just show up and get a participation ribbon and expect that other people are going to pat you on the head, because whether it's Korea or Japan or a domestic competitor, somebody's out there to get ahead of you. And if you've been enjoying a free ride, that's not sustainable. Don't believe me? Only about 10 percent of the original 1955 list of Fortune 500 companies remain on the list today. The rest have gone bankrupt or were merged or acquired, or their growth slowed or declined, causing them to drop off the list. Yes, the titans of industry can drop like flies in a relatively short period of time.

You can *make* it sustainable, however, by always being ahead of the curve. How do you stay hungry when you've succeeded? That's a classic dilemma. How did Bill Belichick keep the New England Patriots on top for so many years? By not allowing them to become complacent. By reminding them that if they weren't hungry enough to keep winning, someone else would cut them out. And I think the same mindset works for business enterprises. (Time will tell what Bill Belichick's new coaching endeavor at the University of North Carolina will do to his remarkable legacy.)

*   *   *

At this point, I'd like to talk about risk management—and risk aversion.

Of course, I myself experience fear of failure. I think we all do. But it's not prominent in my mind when I'm assessing risk. If my gut is saying, *Go ahead and take this risk*, then that is what I do.

So I do have fear of failure . . . but it's not *paralyzing* fear. It's healthy fear, the fear that keeps you from doing stupid things. Even though you may have a very fast, powerful car, you have to be smart about where to let the engine out and where not to. In a business context, that means you keep adequate cash reserves to fight another day if necessary, versus doubling down on every bold, risky move you get an urge to make.

In a way, that's not so much fear of failure as it is respect for the *possibility* of failure, and an incentive to maximize your chances of *not* failing. I have that respect—that *fear* of failure—but it's not an emotion that dominates me at any time; I don't allow myself to become paralyzed by it, or paranoid. When I played lacrosse in high school and college, I tended to play well in important games.

But as an entrepreneur, you have to have a little fear. When I was working with Omelet's CEO and CFO to manage the company's cash flow during two years of losses, we could have doubled down on risky strategies in hopes that the company would quickly turn around . . . and then we might have gone bust. But we didn't do that. We kept hiring to a minimum and cut costs in every area we could in order to live to fight another day—and *then* see where it might be beneficial to go "pedal to the metal." During those difficult financial periods, the guideposts were what people and resources were required to do impeccable work for current clients and what resources were required for successful new business development. Everything else was subject to cutting.

Again, you have to have a healthy fear of taking foolish risks, but we're not talking about jumping off a cliff without a parachute. That's an example of being imprudent with risk. There's no skill in just being foolish or reckless. Remember that scene in *The Deer Hunter* when they're playing Russian roulette? They put one bullet in one chamber of the pistol, and then they spin the cylinder, and there's a one in six chance that whoever pulls the trigger is going to blow his brains out—and the guys at the table are *betting* on it. That's not smart.

I never really believed it when I told myself, *This will be fine; what's the worst that can happen?* I think that approach to risk management does work for some people: *I'll just rebuild my company if this doesn't work out. I'll get into something else,* or *I don't want to go through the pain of a divorce, but if she leaves me I can just get remarried.*

But there's a certain freedom in acknowledging the possibility of failure—and then forging ahead anyway. To be overly fearful of failure can cloud your decision-making. It will make you too risk-averse and it will limit your upside. (It will limit your downside, too, of course, but people who calculate risk in that way shouldn't be entrepreneurs in the first place.)

Dan Sullivan (not the US senator from Alaska, but the entrepreneur and consultant who runs Strategic Coach) has a concept he calls "guesses and bets." As Sullivan sees it, every decision in life is either a guess or a bet. If it's a bet, that means you've actually put some thought into it; if it's a guess, that means you're just taking a shot. I believe that's right, and I think you can decrease your fear of failure by making bets instead of guesses.

If you failed, you can have peace of mind because you made a reasonable bet based on all the data you had and what your gut told you. If you're a disciplined blackjack player, if you follow a really proven system and don't deviate from it, you're going to win more than the average schmo, but you almost certainly won't win that absurd hand on which you take a card, even though you already have nineteen and somehow you think you're going to draw a deuce.

You should constantly be toggling risk-return in your head, but you must also let yourself listen to your gut. (We'll talk more about listening to your gut in the next chapter.) If you're doing that, your fear of failure should be very reasonable and manageable. Understand that *you're going to experience failure sometimes*.

Now, the magnitude of failure you're looking at should also affect your thinking about risk. *I am going to go bankrupt,* or *I'm going to die* is a different calculus from *Okay, I'm going to buy this stock and not that stock*, or *I'm going to switch jobs, but I can probably always go back to my old job if it doesn't work out*. I mean, there's long-tail risk like Armageddon, and then there's day-to-day stuff, and your gut has to weigh the magnitude of a potential loss before letting you take a risk that could lead to Armageddon.

A good example of this thinking in action is how Omelet has addressed investment in AI. Even though we were facing a difficult financial period, we put a quarter of a million dollars of hard costs, plus substantial senior staff time, into development expenses to customize a large language model for the consulting and advertising businesses. We were ahead of the curve and were clearly on to something that might be a game changer. We filed for a patent and created beta models that proved our thesis.

But with the core business struggling, our source of internal cash flow was highly limited, and it became clear that to really build out our proprietary AI model would ultimately require millions of dollars. And then it became clear that many deep-pocketed companies like Open AI, Microsoft, Amazon, and Google, as well as well-funded startups, were investing heavily in a variety of AI applications. We explored raising out-side capital, but the cost was too high and the process too long.

So we stopped funding this venture. The risk/reward equation became unfavorable. We needed to put our scarce cash into growing our core business (Omelet is totally self-funded, with no outside capital sources).

And in fact, we have turned around our core business, and our knowledge of AI has been a critical part of that as we have revamped our internal processes to make ourselves more efficient, lowering costs and enhancing our final work product. We don't have a billion-dollar valuation, which potentially could have resulted if we'd gone all in, raised as much money as we could, and become a leader in AI. But that bet would likely have driven our core business into the ground. We determined that it was not a bet worth taking, so we stopped, fully understanding our substantial sunk cost.

You also have to keep factoring in new data when you're making your bets. You're constantly recalculating. It's not a static process. Every second, theoretically, more data emerges that can change the probabilities. Your gut knows this, and so should your conscious self.

When it manifests as risk aversion, the fear of failure is a mental bias, just like recency bias or confirmation bias or the gambler's fallacy or any of those kinds of cognitive traps. There are mental shortcuts people use instead of taking a rational approach to things. We're not rational beings, and sometimes we overemphasize the positive or the negative. *It'll be okay if I sleep with her—no one will ever know*, or *I'll be okay if I take this drink*, or *I'll win the lottery if I buy this ticket*. Or, on the other hand, *I can't ask her out; I know I'm not her type*, or *I can't apply for that job; they're probably looking for someone more qualified*. Some of us don't want to look at the downsides of the actions we're considering, and others can't see any possible upsides.

Risk aversion (i.e., fear of failure) is a natural human impulse, encoded in our DNA by hundreds of thousands of years of natural selection. Primitive man had to be careful in the choices he made, because in the world of that era, if you made a mistake, a saber-toothed tiger would eat you.

In the twenty-first century, however, we're not talking about life-or-death choices in most situations. We're talking about managing a business, or making (relatively) low-stakes decisions about how to deal with your life. But we're living twenty-first century lives with brains that evolved in 500,000 BC—and those brains are designed to make certain kinds of cognitive errors. Some of us are wired to fear failure intensely, and others are wired not to take the possibility of failure into account. And depending on your wiring, if you don't stop to examine every situation rationally, your confirmation bias will dictate how you respond to the data you think you see. Confirmation bias (a subject I'll discuss a bit further in the next chapter), has a way of screwing up your gut algorithm, because you naturally don't want to *not* believe what you already believe, and you instinctively want to select data to reinforce that belief. That's very dangerous, and it's something you must be on guard against.

There's a difference between being risk averse and just being timid, and risk aversion itself can sometimes be dangerous. Recall when we discussed long-term savings strategies. You might say, "I'm going to keep my money in a savings account when inflation is 4 percent and it's paying 1 or 2 percent." You *think* you're being risk averse because you won't lose your principal—it's insured, after all.

But you're paying tax on that small amount of interest, and your purchasing power is declining because of inflation, so you're actually taking a risk that you're going to retire with not enough money. And yet, most people have their 401(k) in investments that are far too conservative, including young people, who should be 100 percent in diversified stocks.

A friend of mine recently related something he was told by his girlfriend's father, who came up in the 1950s. The gentleman said that after World War II, everybody knew that if you wanted to have a job for life, you went to work for the railroads. That was probably true back then—certainly, that was how everybody thought. But then the interstate highway system was built, and trucking started to take over the freight business. And then, as jet travel advanced, air cargo became viable as yet another competitive pressure on the railroads, and a job with Union Pacific was suddenly no more secure than any other kind of job.

The lesson here is that you can't risk-manage your way through life. You can avoid making foolish mistakes, like not wearing your seatbelt or smoking three packs of cigarettes a day, to manage your risk. But not all of life's risks can be managed—or even predicted—and by trying to avoid all of them, all the time, you run a different kind of risk—you risk missing opportunities.

*   *   *

In his 2016 book, *The Power of Broke*, author and entrepreneur Daymond John advises us to "be in the efforts business."[22] Don't be in the results business, he says, because you can control your effort, but you cannot control your results. That's definitely been my experience—and it's also a way to be more at peace with yourself.

Throughout your life, you have to toggle risk-return. The upside versus the downside. Where is the equation most favorable? That is the ultimate equation that the algorithm in your gut is trying to solve. Should I sleep with this girl? It's going to be a lot of fun, but will my wife find out? Should I stay and have one more drink? Is there a chance I'm going to get a DUI or get in an accident going home? Should I play one more hand of blackjack . . . and make a really big bet this time? Do I start this venture and leave a well-paying job? Am I ready? Do I have enough capital?

The spreadsheets can tell you a lot, but ultimately, the answer comes from working out this equation in your gut . . . if you let yourself listen to it. If the risk you're contemplating is a bad one—a foolish risk, based on a realistic calculation of the odds, the consequences of betting wrong, and the potential gain—your gut will say, *Hmm . . . I'm uneasy. Maybe this is not a good idea, even though the numbers say it is.*

During all that litigation with EMAK, my gut was telling me, *Don't do this.* And I *heard* it, but I was too proud to listen. I did not want anyone to think I was bluffing. That was a very powerful feeling—and it was also wrong. I knew better, but I ignored what my gut was telling me. And my gut was clearly right, as it virtually always is.

So, in order to help you avoid making the same kind of mistake, in the next chapter I'm going to go into detail about when, how, and why you should listen to your gut.

CHAPTER FOURTEEN

Listen to Your Gut Now or
Listen to Lawyers and Judges Later

WE ALL HAVE THIS FUNNY FEELING SOMETIMES. YOU MIGHT HAVE a conversation with your spouse or your brother or a colleague or a doctor, and there's nothing specifically wrong with the conversation . . . but you walk away uneasy. They left something unsaid, or you didn't bring up some topic you really should have raised. Or there was something you couldn't put your finger on that was just . . . not right.

Or maybe you're about to make an investment that looks really good on paper, but something about it feels . . . wrong. Or you find yourself reluctant to go on a first date with someone even though you're attracted to them. You could explore this feeling to determine why you're having it—or you could push it down and hope it goes away, because it's not pleasant.

That feeling is your gut talking to you, and if you're like most people, you don't always listen to it. For many years, I would push my gut away whenever it spoke to me. But I've learned again and again—the hard way—to embrace whatever my gut is saying, because there is virtually always truth in it. It's an uncomfortable feeling: *Uh-uh, this is not a good idea*. That feeling cautions you against sleeping with someone you just met, or it warns you off a bad business deal or a risky investment. The desire to avoid listening to your gut is particularly pronounced when there is pressure from peers or colleagues to go along with the crowd.

And I've found it's almost always right. I call it my *gut algorithm*, and it's a superpower to be able to listen to it, because it enables you to avoid problems, or at least to better understand the risk of an action you're contemplating.

But we tend to ignore it because listening to it doesn't feel good.

* * *

So, how does your gut speak to you? For me, there's a funny feeling, and I know when it's definitely my gut, because it comes from the stomach. When that feeling appears, I've learned to look inward and say, *Why do I feel this way?*

I sometimes overrule my gut. I subordinate it and ignore it and just power through that feeling—and that is always a big mistake. It's like getting a toothache and saying, "I'm not going to the dentist! I hate the Novocain and I hate the drill, and maybe it's really not a cavity. Maybe it's just the weather or something that's making it ache."

But your gut knows better: it *is* a cavity, and it's going to get worse, and you are going to need a root canal if you don't do something.

The consequences of ignoring your gut algorithm extend far beyond physical discomfort, of course. That's where the lawyers and the judges come in, because when you dismiss your gut feelings, you can find yourself in unnecessary legal trouble. Now, by that I don't mean you go rob a bank and get arrested or anything like that. No, you usually just end up as a plaintiff in some kind of needless civil litigation—which is a preview of hell. It can drag on for years, and you just keep doubling down . . . and then, if your opponent is wealthy and/or vindictive, you realize you can't win. You have opened Pandora's Box, and now find yourself not just a plaintiff, but also a defendant in various meritless—but expensive—counter-suits.

* * *

There have been many times in my life when I should have listened to my gut and didn't. For example, when that family friend introduced me to an investment banker to underwrite EMAK's IPO—and then decided to pursue litigation against me and EMAK when we had profoundly different views on what his fee should be. My gut told me very clearly as the process unfolded, *Just use a different banker that he didn't introduce me to, and avoid the potential acrimony and drama.*

But my pride overwhelmed it. *Screw him*, I thought, *I am not going to be extorted. The underwriter will indemnify me and the company, so I have no financial downside.*

I could have used other bankers, but I used Josephthal just to prove my point—and it was a huge mistake. I had a very unpleasant IPO—an event that should have been an occasion of joy—because he filed the lawsuit right at the IPO. All that unpleasantness was easily avoidable, but my pride overruled my gut, and that was a foolish thing.

As bad as that was, however, the cost was just emotional, not financial. The EMAK boardroom debacle ten years later was worse; it cost me enormously, both financially and emotionally. And it was my pride, again, that was responsible: "I am right and they're wrong. They fired me from my own company, and now the company's going to tank. All my net worth is in it, and I have to take it back."

When EMAK let me go, if I'd just embraced my success over the fifteen-year period with the company, I could have saved myself a world of grief. The press release announcing my departure glowed with praise for the "mutual decision to leave after fifteen years with the company." I had a great severance package and was being pursued by top executive search firms and private equity companies for exciting new opportunities. And initially I did embrace it, choosing to remain on the board of directors, but then the stock started really heading downward, key executives started exiting the company, and some EMAK employees started whispering in my ear and stroking my ego: "Oh Don, you need to do something. Only *you* can turn this around. I wish you'd come back."

My gut didn't fall for all that stuff, but my pride jumped up and dragged me into battle. I should have just said, "You know what? I had a really good fifteen-year run. I am proud of all we accomplished. While I don't agree with the direction of the company now, it is time for my next chapter."

It's not like I needed to win that fight for the sake of my career or my future financial prospects. I was very marketable; I was in my upper forties, close to fifty—and that's the prime CEO age. I don't know how much money I could have banked, but as I said, I had a really good severance deal. I had a lot of options, and the public portrayal of my exit was very positive. I could easily have just ridden off into the sunset while strategically selling my EMAK stock.

I remember the bad gut feelings, despite my optimistic calculus: *I can get the company back and be a hero to the shareholders and employees!* I didn't listen to my gut when it told me about all the negativity I would have to go through and about the reality of fighting with a company backed by a billionaire who I felt could hire as many lawyers as needed to make my life miserable. And with civil litigation, even if I won, the appeal process would take months to file, and then there were hearings, new depositions, new data requests, and on and on we would go. Of course, while all this went on—for years—the company was distracted, and performance inevitably suffered. And as the largest common stockholder, I got hit the most from the shares continuing to decline.

I had that gut feeling before I started the hedge fund as well. My friend Solomon, an investment guy whom I really liked, had been trying to launch this fund, but he couldn't get funding. And then, while I was in the middle of starting the EMAK litigation, he said to me, "Let's do this!"

I wanted to go to work again as an entrepreneur, and hedge funds in 2006 were seen as tickets to enormous wealth. They seemingly couldn't do anything wrong, and I was convinced that Solomon had some incredible proprietary model. But while I had a strong finance background, I really wasn't qualified to judge it, and my friends who *were* qualified told me,

"It's not as low-risk as you think, and there are things that can happen." (None of *them* were willing to invest in it!)

Nevertheless, I put five million bucks of precious liquidity into this hedge fund, even though my gut was saying, *I don't really understand this very well, and while I have expertise in finance, my background is not in the hedge fund world.*

To put that kind of liquidity in while I was entering litigation and had no substantive income was just stupid, and my gut was telling me that . . . but I didn't want to disappoint Solomon, who was a dear friend, so I went ahead. Again, it was my pride talking. I wanted to prove to the EMAK people that they hadn't beaten me, and that I was already off to my next big thing. But my gut was telling me, *You don't understand the risk well enough.*

And I didn't.

* * *

I'm not saying my gut was always right, though I cannot recall an incident when it was wrong. When I didn't follow my gut, I was usually headed for trouble. I still remember the bad gut feelings that accompanied all of those decisions. In fact, even writing these chapters about subordinating my gut instincts is highly unpleasant.

During a recent conversation about gut feelings, a friend of mine said, "I always thought it was bad Mexican food." He was joking, of course, but there's some truth to the idea. It's not for nothing that they call it your "gut." As I said earlier, that feeling comes from your stomach—more often than not, there's a real physical sensation you feel down there when you're weighing your options in a high-stakes situation. There really does seem to be an intelligence in your stomach lining, and it knows things.

The Gemini Advanced AI engine responds to a prompt regarding mind/gut connection as follows: "Yes, your gut and mind are directly and intricately linked through a complex bidirectional communication network often referred to as the gut-brain axis. This means that not only does your brain influence your gut, but your gut also significantly impacts your brain function, including your thoughts, emotions, and mental health." (This is a summary of a much more detailed response that delves into the physiology of the gut/mind connection.)

In light of this, when your gut is trying to tell you something and you refuse to listen, the dissonance manifests in physical ways. For some people it's ulcers; for others, like me, it was chronic neck and back pain. That pain is caused by suppressing your knowledge of the inevitable; as I said in Chapter 12, some people pay attention to what they already know, and some don't.

My physical and mental health are much better now (notwithstanding my recent back surgery, which was the culmination of many years of contact sports), because I finally absorbed the lesson I'm now trying to teach you: You ultimately have to listen to your gut, or you will be unhealthy and unhappy. In truth, I love to delve into my gut feelings now, as there is so much wisdom to inform pending important decisions.

*   *   *

A great idiom captures what you're doing when you ignore your gut algorithm: *painting red flags green*. There's a flashing red caution light in your head but you choose to ignore it, so you disconnect the flasher and you proceed despite the high, *high* likelihood that you're making a mistake. (Sure, you can always get lucky. I told you about that guy in traffic school who was the one guy in a thousand who benefitted from not wearing a seatbelt because he was thrown from the car and the car blew up. But that's not a smart decision, because 99 percent of the time, if there's a red flag, it is up for a good reason.)

One circumstance in which people frequently paint red flags green is when they're looking at a financial model. Whatever may be wrong with your business, you can always change a few assumptions and make it look good, right? Plenty of companies, both public and private, do that—and some of them get sued because they are too optimistic, and their investors end up losing money because they believed an unrealistic forecast.

Take mergers and acquisitions, for example: you can make any M&A deal look good. "Oh, we're going to cut 20 percent of the combined workforce, or 20 percent right off the top, and we're going to cross-sell all these services because we do *this* and they do *that*, and they're going to introduce us to their clients and we're going to introduce our [yadda-yadda-yadda] . . ."

You know how that kind of spiel goes. Your engineered financial modeling says, "We can afford to pay a lot for this company because . . . look at the upside!" (Or more realistically, the current business is trending poorly and we need to make a bold move to try to reverse the negative trajectory.) The truth, however, is that it's very hard to justify paying a valuation premium on top of all the legal and accounting fees to close the deal. Not to mention the risk of the current business falling off a cliff because the management team is distracted by the deal.

If you really want to get that deal done, you can *make* the numbers work—and I can't tell you how many bad mergers and acquisitions there are because people do that. The investment bankers want to get paid, so they support whatever foolish, un-gut-checked financial model you sign up for. A friend of mine currently has a banker who is all over him saying, "We can sell your company for a lot of money! We have numerous buyers lined up!"

"I don't see how," this friend confided when he came to me for advice. "I mean, we've lost money for two years in a row. And yeah, we're projecting profitability this year, but until we *know* we're going to be profitable and make at least several million dollars, I wouldn't even *think* of going to market, because that's how you get busted deals, and it's expensive, and it creates turmoil.

"And the banker goes, 'No, no, no—look at this,' and he sends me these detailed models, and they look good. He's using my projections and then using comparables to determine valuation multiples and says, 'This is what we can do,' and he's got good connections in the Middle East and Asia."

I said to him, "Sure, you can make the models work, but that's the same thing as telling your gut, 'No, no, you're wrong.' Your gut is telling you to not allow yourself to get swept up in what Wall Street calls 'deal heat.'"

Be on the lookout: once you get deal heat, the sunk-cost fallacy will rear its ugly head as you start spending more and more time and money on a deal that you don't want to "waste."

* * *

As I said, I used to shut the door on my gut when it told me something I didn't want to hear. Now I try to welcome it—and I'll give you a great example. My decision to go ahead with this book came from my gut. Every analytical bone told me not to do it right now, but just wait to see what happens with my alimony settlement negotiations and imminent remarriage, and after that wait and see how my back is rehabbing. "All of those costs are very large," my left brain said. "Why do you have to do this book *now*? Wait a while, until your cash flow is more certain and you have more time on your hands."

And that is the correct analytical thinking . . . but my gut said, "No, this is the right time. Who knows what the future will bring? Maybe you'll get run over by a car tomorrow and the book will never get written. Or maybe the company will suddenly go under and you won't do it. So go ahead, just go for it. I don't care how busy you are or how much financial pressure you are under."

So my gut isn't always risk averse. Throughout most of this chapter, I've presented scenarios in which the gut tends to advise you to proceed with caution: "Don't go skiing on *that* mountain! You're not that good! The downside is you'd probably break your neck or break your leg, and the upside is not really very high."

But in this case it said, "Go ahead. You will benefit from this, so take the risk. This book can provide real value to its readers and open up totally new horizons for you."

Whenever your gut talks to you, it's something important, even if you don't recognize it. But I don't say, "Okay, I'm about to enter a business transaction—let me ask my gut what I should do." The gut shows up when it needs to. Just as you can't will an erection, you can't will your gut to weigh in. It just shows up. I don't know what that is or how it works, and I don't know how you could even do research on it, because you can't just make the gut *appear*. It pops up when it pops up. You just have to have an open line of communication, and it will talk to you when it needs to.

In matters of health, your gut speaks to you through your body itself. That is especially true with injury for an athlete . . . and I don't think I followed that when I was playing lacrosse. I came back four months after I tore my ACL even though my gut was saying, "You're not ready for the rigor of playing championship level lacrosse. I don't care what the trainer is telling you." And I wasn't ready, particularly at that time, when we were entering the playoffs and the intensity level was ratcheted up even higher.

So listen to your body, and if it says you should take a day off, then take the day off. And if your hammy is really tight, don't sprint today.

Of course, listening to your body is comparatively easy; it speaks a lot louder than your gut does. It also provides important data, usually in the form of pain—and from that we can conclude that sometimes, you have enough data that you don't really *have* to listen to your gut. You already know that eating the whole wedding cake is probably not a good idea, or that avoiding seed oils is better for you. You don't always need your gut, because sometimes the question confronting you is not a gut thing—it's a knowledge thing. You don't need your gut to answer the question, "Do I need another shot of tequila tonight?" You already know the answer.

So I don't find that health issues are much of a gut thing for me (which feels funny to say, since nowadays they say that gut health is supposedly the key to your life). I'm aware of what's healthy and what's not, and I will sometimes choose to do things that are not smart health-wise—we all do. But it's not because I'm subordinating my gut. We all know that having that third serving of mac 'n' cheese is going to lead to a bellyache. You know you need to get a good night's sleep (another thing that can't be willed!) in order to function well. You don't need your gut to tell you that.

* * *

Is there ever a time when it's appropriate to overrule your gut? I don't think so, but if you do overrule it, overrule with full awareness of what your gut is telling you. Perhaps it's not always exactly right. You have to decipher it and dig deeper sometimes.

Then you have to probe the cause of that feeling. You have to say, "Okay, *why* am I uneasy? Is it because of *this*?" Your gut is not like a fortune cookie that comes out of your mouth and you read it and it says, "Don't do this." It's just a feeling, and you have to get good at exploring what that feeling means.

Sometimes experts will tell you your gut is wrong—and they should know, right? Your lawyer or your business advisor tells you to do something, and they're smart, you respect their judgment, *and you are paying them a lot of money* . . . but it doesn't align with your gut.

People get kind of dazzled by their professional advisors, be they doctors, lawyers, or financial planners: "I feel uneasy, but this guy must know what he's talking about—he's a professional!"

For most of my life, that was the circumstance in which I was quickest to dismiss my gut feelings. In hindsight, that was a particular problem in litigation, because the incentive for lawyers is that they get paid when there's more work, and I think I listened to them too much.

Don't get me wrong; I'm not saying lawyers are all so cold-hearted that they'll try to keep you in litigation just so they can keep billing. But they might paint an overly rosy picture of your odds of winning (although they'll be careful not to guarantee anything, obviously).

It's not like they won't settle if you feel you need to settle, but some will feed the ego-driven part of you that aligns with their incentives. If your opponent's lawyer is very aggressive and they file multiple motions and send inflammatory emails, you want *your* lawyer to say, "Well, screw them! Let's countersue!" And you're prone to want to do that for the same reasons *I* wanted to do that: pride, anger, and ego.

They'll convince themselves that what they're doing is in your best interest because they don't want to have a self-image of someone who just milks a client . . . but they don't have all the data your gut has, and you have to let your gut have the last word.

It's one of life's inevitabilities: from time to time you're going to get business advice or legal advice you don't think is right. And in one sense, you *have* to rely on your advisors . . . but in another sense, you have to weigh their advice carefully.

Of course you're not wrong to think, *I'm paying a lot of money for them. They're smart, and they're more experienced than I am. Maybe I should just listen to them.*

But they sometimes lack all the relevant data regarding what is really going on in your life. They're not a substitute for your gut. Your gut only cares about your best interest.

Let me say that again. Your gut only cares about your best interest. It doesn't care about sparing your ego (even though it will factor that in). It doesn't care about the lawyer's billable hours or the doctor's expertise with the operation he thinks you should have. It just cares about your well-being. Your gut is virtually always right—and if your gut is saying, "Stop, all you're doing is escalating the litigation, and it's going to cost you another fifty grand," you should listen.

At the end of the day, you are your own lawyer, you are your own business advisor, and you are your own healthcare provider. And ultimately, you get penalized for substituting other peoples' judgment for your gut when deep down, you know what you need to do. Your gut is your best advisor, and nobody else is even close—not your parents, not your spouse. Nobody.

When you look at how people negotiate and judge risk-return, there's a whole spectrum of approaches, but my experience is that your gut algorithm is the best calculator. That doesn't mean it's always 100 percent right—it's all a question of probabilities. By definition, any risk has an uncertain outcome. Situations are dynamic and can change quickly. But truly being in touch with your gut will always give you the most favorable odds to realize the best possible outcome. Remember, it's your business. It's your health. It's your life. Trust the advice of your most loyal and dedicated partner, the one who will always have your back—your gut.

CHAPTER FIFTEEN

Don't Make Enemies

It may seem obvious, but I'll say it anyway: One important thing you can do to increase your chances of success in life is try not to make enemies.

Instead, you need to get people on your side, and get them to want you to succeed. The way you do that is by being a generally good person and not screwing people over. Be candid and honest, even when it's not easy, and help people without any expectation for something in return.

Why you do this matters, of course, but what matters more is that you *do it*—for whatever reason. You can do it because you believe in karma, or because some of the people you're interacting with today may, in the future, be in a position to give you a break, or they may say a good thing about you to an influential person, or they may introduce you to your future wife or husband.

Or you can do it simply because that's just the way the world works best—and frankly, it's the only way to live without a lot of anger and a lot of angst. Not having enemies is just a better way to live. You'll get farther, and you'll have a more pleasant life.

* * *

Of course, there's no way for even the most agreeable person to go through their entire life making no enemies at all. The world is an imperfect place, and there are bad people out there who do bad things—and can do bad things to you. They might do them maliciously, or they could have so many personal problems that you're just collateral damage.

Either way, you can't be so pliant that you think, *Okay, this guy just punched me in the face and stole my girlfriend, but I don't want to upset him, so I'm not going to do anything about it.* That's not a good way to not make enemies; that's just being a patsy and a doormat.

Some people will always be determined to make an enemy of you—especially if you're successful—because jealousy is a very powerful emotion. You're dating the girl they wanted, or you have the job they wanted, or you're popular, and they're resentful. And I've learned that there's no way to placate those kinds of people. I used to try to go out of my way to "nice" them to death. It doesn't work. They just sense weakness, and then they become even more aggressive.

Generally, however, what people do and say about you is not about you; it's about them, and internalizing this has made my life much more pleasant.

Say you're driving on the highway, and somebody cuts you off. Your first instinct may be to give them the finger, or to honk at them, which is my instinct. What an inconsiderate jerk!

But maybe it's not about you at all. Maybe their wife is having a baby and they're taking her to the delivery room. Maybe they've just had a terrible day. Whatever it is, it's usually not about you.

And even if it is somehow about you—so what? A random person on the freeway was rude to you. They're just an obnoxious driver . . . and how much capital in your brain are you going to waste on that?

So try not to judge, and try to have some empathy. Give others the benefit of the doubt: it's an easier way to deal with people, and it helps you not take it personally.

That applies to social and professional situations as well. Sometimes there's someone in your orbit whom you can't avoid, and friction develops between you. But even then, it's not necessarily about you. Maybe it's a misunderstanding, or the person is having a bad day, or maybe it's jealousy or envy connected to work or a potential romantic partner.

Of course, sometimes they're just a jerk, and when you find yourself in conflict with someone like that, you don't need to respond. I've made the mistake of reflexively responding to people's aggressive behavior, and it rarely leads to a good outcome. You can't seek justice in every interaction with people; you will not get it, and you will drive yourself crazy in the attempt. Instead, you can simply choose to not associate with them. My experience is when you ignore jerks, they then want to win you over, and the entire power dynamic shifts.

Don't ever say anything negative about them, though. In my experience, there is no upside to that—and besides, people will admire you if you don't trash-talk others, even when they're trash-talking you. You'll get more respect by being the bigger person, whereas if you become known as someone who trashes others when they're not around, people will start to think that maybe *you're* the jerk. So just don't do it.

Of course, if there's a serious conflict, you have to address it. Don't *trash* them, but do confront them in a professional way that makes your position clear: "Listen, I don't know what your problem is. If you want to talk about it, I'm happy to, but I'm telling you, *don't* do that again." You've got to figuratively punch the bully in the nose, because a bully is someone you rarely can negotiate with.

That kind of confrontation is a last resort, but it always works. They'll realize that messing with you is not a smart thing for them to do . . . and they may even acquire a newfound respect for you, like that guy I mentioned in Chapter 10, who was nasty to me no matter what I did or said. He was senior to me, but I was kind of a rising star, and I think he resented that. The more I tried to be nice, the worse it got, until I finally said, "Listen, buddy, I don't know what your problem is, but if you want to talk about it, I'm willing to listen . . . or just stay out of my way and I'll stay out of your way." And within a month, he became my best friend in that office.

It's important to remember that the vast majority of people are not jerks. You have to have empathy for everyone and try to find common ground somehow. That's how I try to connect with people who disagree with me politically; I remind myself that people who don't agree with me can still be kind, decent, and smart people. I have some relatives I relate to in that way. I think they're misguided in what they believe, but I don't think they have character flaws or are in any way evil. And by having difficult conversations in a respectful manner, we can sometimes even change one another's minds. Think about some of the strongest opinions you hold: you probably know a few people who disagree vehemently with one or more of those views. But if you respect that person, couldn't there be something they could say that might change your mind? In other words . . . is it possible *you're* the one who's wrong? In the vast majority of cases, I find that there actually is a fair amount of common ground shared by most of us, but we allow sound bites and tribe membership to obscure it. And, of course, politicians and the media have a vested interest in promoting conflict.

The same goes for interpersonal conflicts. You have to understand that there are two sides to every story; try to find some common ground, and then make a judgment. What's worth it, what's not? This was one reason I ultimately realized that my EMAK battle had to stop, even though I believed I was right—not just because I couldn't afford to keep litigating, but because the years were ticking by, and the people on the other side, some of whom were very smart and decent people, didn't think I was right.

*   *   *

If you do have someone in your life who falls into the category of *enemy*, you should do your best to mend fences with them. It could be a problematic relationship in your family, or maybe a friend you haven't spoken to in years, or somebody you used to work with. That was another of the reasons I ultimately dropped my litigation with EMAK. I didn't apologize, because there was nothing to apologize for, but I realized there was no point in carrying this ugly, permanent enmity around for the rest of my life.

Depending on that person's current proximity to your life (if they live in Mongolia now and you don't have a summer place there and you don't travel to Asia all the time, there's probably no need or reason to contact them), my advice would be to reach out and clear the air, especially if it's a relative or someone who hops into your social circle at least once a year. Whether it's somebody at work, a neighbor, a former friend who's still in your social circle, or a relative who shows up at family events . . . if there is any reason that you're going to have to continue to interface with someone, you should try to clear the air. You don't have to admit you're wrong or seek some confession from your antagonist; just reach out and try to find some common ground. In many cases, you will not speak to that person again for another year or two, but the tension will be gone.

And they'll appreciate it because they are likely thinking the same thing but don't have the courage to approach you—or their pride is too great for them to reach out. So just take the initiative and say, "Hey, how are you doing? I'm sorry we've had these issues, but I'd be happy to talk about it. I just want you to know it was nothing personal." Usually I find that the other person is incredibly grateful when I do that, because they want to clear the air as well, and I feel good about it afterward.

So think about who you might want to mend fences with, and take action. Don't wait until they're on their deathbed; just do it. By taking the initiative, you are not compromising your principles; you are conserving your emotional energy for more important current and future endeavors.

* * *

There's a certain personality type that thrives on conflict and chaos . . . and I don't know how those people function. What's the upside?

Can you succeed that way? Sure, we can all cite examples of people who will never be up for sainthood but who get great results. Yet they tend to make lots of enemies on their climb to the top. And if they're in the public eye, other people see that behavior and start to think that's the way you have to operate if you want to make things happen. They get the message that in order to succeed, you need really sharp elbows—and I'm saying you don't.

Business is not a zero-sum game. There's room for an infinite number of entrepreneurs, depending on the quality of their ideas, as long as the economy is growing and there's capital available. There's an infinite land-scape of opportunities, so reaching the horizon doesn't require you to take other people down. There's room for an infinite number of successes. If you don't get that promotion to CEO, you should still applaud the person who does.

Now, you might say, "I'm not going to stay at the number two posi-tion for the rest of my career!" Fine—you can look for a job that offers you more opportunity to advance to the position you want. General Electric, in the old days, would hold a competition for the coveted CEO job . . . and then the two or three "losing" finalists would leave and go run some other large, prestigious company and get paid a fortune. As I have repeatedly asserted in this book, accepting and embracing outcomes even when they don't go your way invariably opens up new and more exciting opportuni-ties if you don't "fight the tape."

So go and do that. And after you leave, people will remember that you respected the process. You might not have agreed with the outcome, but you wished the new CEO well. You know how many boards want to hire a person like that, after seeing the way they conducted themselves? You know how many employees want to work for a boss who conducts themself with dignity and respect? The vast majority of people do.

Making enemies is no way to live. There's a qualitative cost to your life. It's not pleasant to have enemies and to think people are out to get you. I don't want to be kept up at night grinding my teeth because someone doesn't like me and doesn't want me to succeed. Moreover, if you're unhappy and resentful, you're not going to perform at your best. You're also not going to be fun to be around. And ultimately, your health will suffer.

Living that way can also make you paranoid and vindictive: *Maybe they're going to call my boss.* Or if I'm running a public company, *maybe they're going to start a rumor to drive the stock price down, so I'd better start planning my revenge now.* Your mind can go to strange places when you're under stress—and having enemies is stressful. On a practical level, there's no upside.

Again, I don't mean to suggest that you can get through life without conflict. But when you're on the opposite side of some issue with someone, it's best to say, "You know what? I don't agree with Michael . . . but he is a good guy. He treats people fairly, and he returns my phone calls. He shows respect, and he's not arrogant. I may not think he deserved that promotion, but I can grudgingly admit he's a standup guy."

Only good things can happen if that's the way you treat people when faced with a difficult situation.

*   *   *

A friend of a friend of mine once lived in the Hollywood Hills, next door to a fairly well-known television actor who recently passed away at the age of ninety. At some point he and his neighbor got into a fight over a tree. ("Those branches are on *my* property!") They fought for years and went to court constantly over this tree, and ultimately my friend's friend died very young, at only sixty-nine. I truly believe having an enemy took years off his life.

These two neighbors—did they start out saying, "My goal is to make my neighbor's life an absolute hellhole"? Sure, there are people like that, but most people aren't. And this is the classic example of the kind of dispute that is easy to avoid.

I'll give you an example. Where I live, there's no fence that separates our property from our neighbors on either side and conforms to the actual property lines. And these lots aren't perfect squares. Now, on one side are trees that have to be maintained that straddle both properties, and on the other side is a drainage ditch—Tennessee gets some really intense rains, and there are drainage issues, so a water system channels the water so it flows out correctly. Now, that ditch is mostly on our property, but the water ends up flowing mostly to the neighbor's property.

So in both cases, we offered to be a good neighbor after we moved into the house. To the neighbor on the tree side of our property, I said, "Hey, we've got to maintain these trees, so I'll split the cost with you." And I approached our other neighbor the same way about the water system.

In both cases, both neighbors decided to just continue to pay for the necessary maintenance work on their own, and they wouldn't take any reimbursement. I think they were just happy that I'd offered to split it and I wasn't looking for a problem. (These neighbors are also clearly wonderful and reasonable people, so my wife and I are very fortunate.)

It's easy to imagine how both situations could have caused trouble. It happens all the time—the civil courts are full of neighbor disputes over utter nonsense. But what an unpleasant way to live, feuding with your neighbor over something stupid. I just won't do it, particularly with a neighbor or family member. My neighbors don't have to be my best friends, but I will not have a dispute. The cost/benefit ratio is too far out of whack. It's just too unpleasant to constantly have to think, *Uh-oh, I don't want to look my neighbor in the eye because we have this thing.* I'm just not going to live that way. And I urge you not to live that way either.

I have found that the best way to avoid personal animosity is to understand that there are two sides to every story, and that the other person may believe their story as fervently as you believe yours. That may baffle you, but it makes a potential dispute less personal. It's not about you; it's about what's right and wrong, and there can be multiple reasonable interpretations of that.

* * *

As with every other attitude adjustment I've recommended in this book, you have to internalize this; you can't just *will* not having enemies—because you can't force *yourself* not to think poorly of someone you don't like. You can't will that out of your mind. You can't will yourself not to feel angry. And because other people are human, just like you are, they in turn can't will themselves not to dislike you.

You can give people no actual reason to *dislike* you, and you can treat them with the respect that they are not necessarily treating you with . . . but ultimately, at the end of the day, you can't control their jealousy, their internal rage, or whatever is driving their animosity toward you.

And you have to be comfortable with that. All you can do is not give them any real reason to consider you an enemy. And if you make a habit of treating everyone that way, the number of actual, true enemies you have will be close to zero.

The best way to minimize the number of enemies you have is to make as many friends as you can. Get people *not* hating you; get them on your side. And one way to do that—as I learned playing lacrosse and football and other sports—is to be a great teammate.

Everyone in a top athletic program is competing for a limited number of spots. Everyone at a place like Hopkins Lacrosse was the star of their high school team. Bar none. But there are only three starting attackmen, six to nine regular midfield players, three starting defensemen, and only one starting goalie. Besides that, ten to fifteen freshmen are recruited every year, and there is now a transfer portal where players from other schools can transfer in and play right away without sitting out a year. And yet, everyone thinks they should be a starter because they were the star in high school. That means there is always potential for jealousy and conflict.

But if you're a great teammate, everyone knows it. The coach knows it. The players know it. And then, when somebody gets injured, you might be the first guy in to fill his spot, *just because* you've been a great teammate. You bust your ass in practice. You don't drag your feet because you're upset that you're not the starter. And eventually, that comes back to you. There have been instances at Hopkins where nonstarters were voted captain because they were such great teammates and exhibited tremendous leadership capabilities.

*   *   *

Finally, it's better to not have enemies because enemies can trip you up when you don't expect it. You just don't know people's networks, and they can come out of the bushes years after they believe you've wronged them in some way, and then that enemy brings you down.

You could make ten friends and one enemy, and then that lowly person you wronged rises up the totem pole—and remembers that you treated them like garbage when the shoe was on the other foot. Somehow, that person you didn't treat with respect, or that person you cavalierly fired—their cousin turns out to be the head of Blackstone Private Equity, and you're looking to get funded by them. And that person you wronged will say to his cousin, "That guy's a skunk; don't give him a damned penny." You just don't know what can result from mistreating people; nothing good can happen, and a lot of bad things can happen. And many times, you won't even know why you didn't close that deal or get that coveted piece of new business. Behind closed doors, someone blows up your company by urging the decision-makers not to close your deal because of your alleged bad character. You aren't in the room and can't defend yourself, so you get the call and the contact gives some general reason you weren't selected, and says only that everyone appreciated your great efforts but they decided to go in another direction.

Have you ever seen the movie *Election*? Matthew Broderick plays Jim McAllister, a teacher who ends up getting fired after fixing an election for student council president. (He's not really the villain of the story; he has reasons for what he does, which I won't get into here.)

His undoing ultimately comes about because he inadvertently makes an enemy of the school janitor. While cleaning out the refrigerator in the faculty lounge, he starts throwing old, rotten food into a trash can—but his attention is on the inside of the fridge, and he's not looking at the trash can, so he misses it when he tosses a carton of old Chinese food. The food splatters all over the floor, and the janitor just happens to be walking by the door and sees it happen. McAllister never notices the spilled food, and the janitor, angry that he's going to have to clean it up, holds a grudge . . . and later sees McAllister throw a ballot away and rats him out for fixing the election. McAllister is fired and his entire life and career are ruined—all because he accidentally made an enemy of a janitor.

* * *

I believe in karma. Maybe it's in this life, or maybe it's the next life, but I do think there's a karmic energy at work in the universe, and that what you put forward comes back to you.

Way back in the early days of EMAK, the puppeteers Sid and Marty Krofft once gave me some good advice when we were looking at promoting one of their puppet shows. They were great guys, and we got along well, and on one occasion when I met with them, I'd had a crappy day. I don't recall exactly what it was—either something bad had happened to a family member or some deal fell through—but I mentioned it because I was feeling a bit sorry for myself.

Sid was a real mensch—they both were—and he said, "You know what? Go to a soup kitchen. Go do something for somebody with no expectation of anything in return. Go do that. That's how you deal with your sadness."

I didn't go to a soup kitchen, but I took his advice to heart. Instead, I called my mother, whom I hadn't spoken to in a week or two. And talking to her took my mind off my problems. She was having problems of her own (health issues), and after listening to her for a while, I suddenly realized that our conversation had changed the entire narrative of my day.

So I'd like to pass that advice along to you. Instead of feeling sorry for yourself, go do something for somebody else. And do it in the right spirit, not because you expect to be karmically rewarded, but because it's the right thing to do. You can't do it in a Machiavellian way—*I'm going to go to the soup kitchen, and now I expect the universe to get my big deal funded because I spent two hours ladling soup.* You just have to do it from the heart.

I think the universe has an invisible hand that guides you if you do your part, and part of doing your part is being a good person. And that's how you can manage not to have a lot of enemies.

CHAPTER SIXTEEN

Final Thoughts

IN THE PAST COUPLE OF YEARS, I'VE FOUND MYSELF ADOPTING an outlook on life that seems counterintuitive to me. I'm getting into the latter years of middle age, a stage of life at which I would think, in general, one would get more depressed. It's a time when you have to face the fear of your mortality. There are ever more everyday aches and pains, and you are fighting the march of time to keep looking your best, and you know it's not going to get any better. At the same time, you also have to face the limits of your ambition: you're never going to be President of the United States, you're not going to be the quarterback of the Dallas Cowboys, and you're not going to be a billionaire if you aren't one already.

And yet, I'm more content and happy than I've ever been.

That contentment was the ultimate driver of my decision to write this book. I've had a pretty wild ride, and all my setbacks were basically self-inflicted, if I look back at them honestly. If I knew then what I know now, I could have avoided a lot of the turmoil, a lot of the expense, and a lot of the heartburn I got . . . and that experience is the gift I want to give to other people, so that maybe they can avoid some of that pain.

When I see a young person falling into these traps, I almost want to shake them and say, "Don't do it! Give it up. Your ego is overwhelming you, and you're going to regret it." Without diminishing the joy of my life and the success I've experienced in my life, I have to acknowledge that I would have been more successful if I could have risen above the kind of negativity I've described in these pages. My hope is that other people, armed with my experiences, can avoid running into the same pitfalls.

But then again, if I didn't go through all that *tsuris*, I might not be where I am now. Omelet, for all its *mishegoss*, brings me a lot of joy . . . and I wouldn't be at Omelet if my hedge fund hadn't blown up . . . and I wouldn't have started the hedge fund if EMAK hadn't blown up.

*   *   *

Throughout my life, I lived with a certain amount of anxiety. Now, however, I'm able to be relatively content in any kind of environment, because I've learned to accept and embrace whatever circumstances I find myself in, and I take comfort in the notion that there is some invisible hand guiding events—a long-term plan that makes sense of it all.

And I don't have to understand what that long-term plan is at any given moment. I just have to do my part and be a good person, and work my ass off at whatever I do, whether it's this book or my business or my marriage. The chips will fall wherever they fall, and everything will ultimately be fine and, in fact, work out for the best. I certainly don't have as much money as I could have, but so what? I am financially secure, with wonderful friends and family and a business that does great work that operates in a manner we are all very proud of.

Even the way I'm dealing with my back recovery is informed by this outlook. Some days, I feel I'm making good progress. Other days, I think, *Damn, I am going to have bad back pain forever.* I don't struggle too much with that, however; it's going to be what it's going to be, and I'll try to do my best to heal it with rigorous physical therapy. Years ago, the "unfairness" of this happening to me would have bothered me a lot more.

Because I've learned this lesson, I am now a relatively happy and content person, and I just wish I could go back in time and get through the thick skull of my younger self so that he could have learned this sooner. I would have had a more peaceful life, and I would have avoided some major downturns in my life and career.

Now, don't get me wrong. I've had a very *good* life. I don't want to say I've been miserable and now all of a sudden the light's come on. That's just not true in any sense. But the underlying anxiety I used to have is largely gone, and it's not because I take Xanax. It's because I've learned to accept and embrace the things that used to make me anxious.

* * *

Throughout the most dramatic and stressful moments of my life—hearing that those kids had died from our Pokémon toys, having my victory over the EMAK board overturned by the Delaware Supreme Court—I have attempted to hold onto a sense of calm, a sense of *well, that has just happened*. My success in doing that back then was more limited, but that is what I have learned to do effectively over the years. Today, I handle adversity with as much calm as one can reasonably expect.

For example, my father recently passed away. Now, he was 101 years old, and he was sick the previous year, so it's not like some horrible, unexpected accident took him in his prime. But it was still a real shock—nothing prepares you for the death of a parent.

All the same, my emotional reaction wasn't unbearable. *Okay, that just happened.* I didn't sugarcoat it to myself—I felt enormous grief, as anyone would—but I didn't have a complete breakdown, either.

My emotional responses are usually very reserved. I don't tend to cry at those moments (though I did at both my mother's and father's funerals). I remember hearing about those two kids' Pokémon deaths in a board meeting, and I didn't even interrupt the meeting. I just excused myself and went to talk to a few people, including our law firm and PR firm, and then very calmly went back into the board meeting. I was deeply impacted by the situation, of course, but rather than gnashing my teeth, I just accepted it . . . and then embraced what had to be done moving forward, including ensuring that the families of those kids were well taken care of.

Now, once again, this is something I want to make sure I've been crystal clear on: To *embrace* something doesn't mean to welcome it happily. It doesn't mean, "Wow, I'm going to celebrate this tragedy because I'm so pleased about it."

Embrace just means, "I've got a lot of difficult work to do to dig this company out from under the tragedy of two kids dying from our toys, from the financial and legal exposure to the possibility of our client firing us, to . . . I don't know, whatever else could happen. And I don't have the option of doing anything else but rolling up my sleeves and getting to work on a series of unpleasant tasks."

In other words, to embrace something is to refuse to avoid it. I embrace the challenge, not the disaster that precipitated it. The embrace I'm talking about here is the embrace of whatever you've got to do because of your reality. Don't wish that you didn't have to do what you have to do, or that your reality was somehow different. It just is what it is.

Any setback in life is a reality that must be confronted. You can't be an entrepreneur for very long and not face lots of setbacks. Your key client leaves you, even though you did nothing wrong. Your most valuable employee leaves you because they want to start their own business and be their own boss. You run out of cash. You have clients who aren't paying. It's just one thing after another, and you have to constantly be embracing what you have to do.

I'll repeat once again because it's such a critical point—that doesn't mean that you're happy about it or that it's a good situation. It's not an embrace of delight; it's an embrace of acceptance. You just have to embrace your challenges and take comfort in the hope that there's some master plan guiding everything, and that as long as you're doing your part, behaving ethically, and working hard, things will turn out as they should. Whatever that outcome turns out to be, you should take comfort in that because you have no choice. Fighting it will be futile. It's like trying to get everyone to like you: it doesn't work, and if you insist on trying to force it to work, you are destined to a life of misery.

I smile now when I think "what if." What if, in late 1997, with EMAK's stock trading near its peak of $30+ per share (over five times its $6 IPO price in 1994), I'd pursued a credible New York Stock Exchange company's takeover offer of "mid-30's" price. I had recently turned forty and could have walked away with well north of $50 million. (And if I'd put $50 million into an S&P 500 index fund at the end of 1997, it would be worth over $300 million today.) After staying on for a transition period, I could have had my pick of CEO jobs or private equity-backed deals, with a bank account large enough to enable me to do whatever I wanted. I was blinded by my belief that our stock would continue its exponential rise, and that I would cash out at some future date with untold wealth. How naive and arrogant.

I don't grind my teeth about that, however. Instead, I laugh at that very real opportunity I declined to pursue, because I accept that my destiny was not to be a big-time mogul flying around in my own private jet. Why, I don't know, but that is the reality of my journey, and I fully accept this. I'm at peace with it.

*   *   *

This realization tends to come about gradually as we get older—which brings me back to the thought I expressed at the start of this chapter. Despite the indignities of age—the inevitable deterioration of the body, the acknowledgement of missed opportunities, the sense of narrowing possibilities—surveys show that senior citizens are generally happier than millennials and "zoomers."

Older people are happier because they've come to a place of acceptance. (I'm not going to become an NFL player!) They are more comfortable with who they are and what they are. They're no longer in the fight to the same degree. They've either "made it" or not made it, and there's a certain peace to that.

Also, family life tends to get easier by this point in one's life; the kids are not young anymore, so you're not squabbling over how to raise them, and if you had a bad marriage, it has probably run its course by this point. You're not trying to keep up with the Joneses, and you are not trying to drag them down to your level, so there's more of a sense of comfort in your own skin.

I always assumed when I was younger that old people lived in terror of the end—you know, "Oh my God, I'm going to die!" But now I accept my mortality, and I really don't think about it much. The end of my days is closer than it once was, and that's just fine with me. I have also come to believe that each human being's soul is eternal, and that when our physical being ceases on earth, our soul manifests in new ways in our next life journey. I believe this to my core. It is a belief that has come to me recently, and has been informed by study with my remarkable Nashville rabbi, Rabbi Yitzchok Tiechtel. My gut says this is true, and this core belief provides enormous comfort as I age.

*　*　*

The brother of an old high school classmate recently called me and said, "Your name came up as a potential nominee for the school's athletic hall of fame."

I didn't know the guy very well, but he interviewed me, and after determining that I was a viable candidate, asked me if I would like to be considered. I'd have to file an application, he said, and then there's a committee that does background research and votes on it.

I don't know how the nominating committee selects people. Obviously they ask around and investigate college and career accomplishments, and I guess they go through record books in the archives. They do it every other year, I'm told. And it's not just athletes—they also induct coaches, administrators, and athletic directors.

I have very fond memories of high school—not just sports, but the whole high school experience. As I look back now, I can see that—pardon the cliché—it really was a special time in my life. Really, it was the *happiest* time in my life in terms of having fun and being anxiety free.

So I said yes, I'd be interested, and it would be a real honor to be voted in.

After I hung up the phone, I was surprised at how excited I was about the call. After all, my time as a lacrosse and football player at Elmont High was fifty years ago. It means a lot to me, especially because I know the school has seen a *lot* of very good athletes come and go over the course of decades, and I'm sure a lot of deserving candidates must have gotten overlooked.

I was formally accepted and have just been inducted into the Elmont Memorial High School Athletic Hall of Fame. The honor is especially gratifying given the fact that I didn't end my lacrosse career at Hopkins in the way I would have liked—as an All-American, or maybe as one of the captains of the team. After the multiple knee injuries and my subsequent decision to leave the team my senior year, this is a reaffirmation of the talent and grit I had when I was at my physical peak.

Elmont Spartans Athletic Hall of Fame Plaque

Elmont Hall of Fame
Induction Ceremony

Elmont Spartans Athletic
Hall of Fame

* * *

There's a phenomenon called *pronoia*, or "reverse paranoia." It's a psychological condition first described in 1982, in which people believe that everyone is saying nice things about them all the time. "Pronoiacs" believe that people who know them are conspiring to do them good, that casual acquaintances are close friends, and that the routine pleasantries people engage in when making small talk are actually genuine expressions of concern and esteem.[23]

Now, I know that pronoia is classified as a mental illness, but I can't help but think that must be a nice way to live, going through your days believing that everyone loves you. Most of us don't have the luxury of that kind of delusion—we get into conflicts, and we even make enemies. It's the nature of the human condition. The best most of us can do is try to see the world with enough good faith and optimism to believe that most people are not out to get us.

I'm not a big Shakespeare fan, but while my editor and I were discussing this chapter, he quoted a line from *Julius Caesar* that struck a chord with me: "The evil that men do lives after them; / The good is oft interred with their bones."[24]

That's a depressing thought . . . but guess what? People remember the good that you do also. You may be pleasantly surprised to find that your accomplishments and the things you've done for others are not forgotten, and they circle back to you in direct and indirect ways. For example, if you treat somebody well when they leave your company because they are just not the right fit—give them a good severance package and try to help them land in a good spot—then they may end up at a Fortune 500 company and become a client someday. Even those folks who choose to leave (sometimes after receiving a big promotion and raise!) should be treated this way. Wish them well and thank them for their service. Only good things can come from that.

I will give you a recent personal example. A few years ago, I received a call from the president of the Johns Hopkins Alumni Association telling me I was being awarded the Johns Hopkins Heritage Award, which is presented periodically to alumni or non-alumni friends of the university for outstanding long-term service. It is one of Hopkins' most prestigious honors, and I had no idea I was being considered. I love the university, and it has been a true honor to serve it any way I can, through various committees, the board of trustees, and by being a consistent and meaningful long-time donor. Somehow, after almost fifty years of service, I was formally recognized. It was a very special day when President Ron Daniels and then–Chair of the Board of Trustees Jeff Aronson presented me with the award.

*The Johns Hopkins University
Heritage Award*

*Twelve Years of Service on the
Hopkins Board of Trustees*

So don't think, just because you haven't been rewarded for something you've done, that nothing good is ever going to come of it, or that people aren't going to notice. You may not have been thanked, and you may not have been given a prize. You may not even have been acknowledged. But people notice . . . and even if they don't, you can still be proud of what you've done because the fact of it still exists in the universe. It didn't just disappear. And given my core belief that one's soul lives on in eternity, your actions on this earth will be reflected in your next journey.

* * *

If I had to choose just one final message for the reader to take away from this book, I'd want you to remember my admonition to accept and embrace everything that happens to you in life, good and bad. That's the main thing I've learned, and it applies to everything you do. It is futile to fight reality, and if you truly accept and embrace reality in your actions, good will come of it, even if it isn't immediately obvious. This is guaranteed.

Every Saturday, I reread my life philosophy, which I documented about two years ago: "Work hard, be kind, take initiative, and then trust as life unfolds. God has a plan that favors me, and I must accept and embrace whatever happens with peace, comfort, gratitude, and happiness." I urge you to adopt this philosophy as your own. Listening to your gut will be your guide in employing this philosophy.

My life up to this point has been an incredible ride, and I find myself truly grateful for my experiences in athletics, in dancing, in my career, and in my relationships. I've finally learned how to be at peace with life's many ups and downs, and it is a wonderful way to live. I sincerely hope that you, too, can find inner peace in your unique life journey.

ENDNOTES

1 "Anthem," by Leonard Cohen, produced by Leonard Cohen, Steve Lindsey, Bill Ginn, Leanne Ungar, Rebecca De Mornay, and Yoav Goren, Columbia, released November 24, 1992.

2 Aldous Huxley, *Collected Essays* (Harper & Row, Publishers, Inc., 1959), 202.

3 *Jackie Mason: The World According to Me,* directed by Dwight Hemion, written by Jackie Mason and Ron Clark, 1988.

4 James Joyce, *Ulysses* (Oxford University Press, 1998), 182.

5 Robert Ringer, *Winning Through Intimidation* (New York: Skyhorse Publishing, 1973).

6 Miguel Angel Ruiz, MD, *The Four Agreements* (San Rafael: Amber-Allen Publishing, 1997).

7 James Dyson, *Against the Odds: An Autobiography* (Texere, 2003).

8 *License to Operate,* directed by James Lipetzky, South Central Los Angeles, Los Angeles, CA: Omelet, 2015.

9 Clayton Christensen, *The Innovator's Dilemma* (Boston: Harvard Business Review Press, 1997).

10 "The Extended Family," See's Candies, accessed September 27, 2025, https://www.sees.com/about-us/corporate.

11 See the classic *Harvard Business Review* article that discusses the concept of "jobs to be done" for your customers. Clayton Christensen, Taddy Hall, Karen Dillon, and David S. Duncan, "Know Your Customers' 'Jobs to Be Done,'" *Harvard Business Review*, September 2016, https://hbr.org/2016/09/know-your-customers-jobs-to-be-done.

12 The lacrosse player, not to be confused with the former NHL executive.

13 US Bureau of Labor Statistics, "35 Percent of Employed People Did Some or All of Their Work at Home on Days They Worked in 2023," July 15, 2024, https://www.bls.gov/opub/ted/2024/35-percent-of-employed-people-did-some-or-all-of-their-work-at-home-on-days-they-worked-in-2023.htm.

14 "The Serenity Prayer," The General Service Board of Alcoholics Anonymous (Great Britain) Limited, accessed September 28, 2025, https://www.alcoholics-anonymous.org.uk/magazines/the-serenity-prayer/#:~:text=%E2%80%9CGOD%20grant%20me%20the%20serenity,resonated%20deeply%20within%20my%20soul.

15 Jerry Wallace, "Essays, Papers & Addresses: Thoughts On Calvin Coolidge: Politician and Office Holder," Coolidge Foundation, August 31, 2007, https://coolidgefoundation.org/resources/essays-papers-addresses-25/.

16 Rumsfeld, Donald. "Strategic Imperatives in East Asia." *Heritage Foundation*, 3 March 1998, https://www.heritage.org/asia/report/strategic-imperatives-east-asia. Accessed January 19, 2026.

17 Adam Hayes, "Fighting the Tape: What It Is, How It Works, Examples," *Investopedia*, updated April 30, 2022, https://www.investopedia.com/terms/f/fightingthetape.asp.

18 "Fram Oil Filter Commercial—1972," May 22, 2012, YouTube video, 0:31, https://www.youtube.com/watch?v=OHug0AIhVoQ.

19 Jake Trotter, "Ohio State Suffers Fourth Straight Loss in Michigan Rivalry," *ESPN*, November 30, 2024, https://www.espn.com/college-football/story/_/id/42701461/michigan-upsets-ohio-state-4th-straight-win-rivalry.

20 Andrew S. Grove, *Only the Paranoid Survive* (New York: Crown Currency, 1999), p. 3.

21 Ibid, p. 117.

22 Daymond John, *The Power of Broke: How Empty Pockets, a Tight Budget, and a Hunger for Success Can Become Your Greatest Competitive Advantage* (New York: Crown Currency, 2016).

23 "Pronoia," Wikipedia, accessed September 28, 2025, https://en.wikipedia.org/wiki/Pronoia_(psychology); Dr. Fred Goldner, "Pronoia," *Social Problems*, October 1982.

24 William Shakespeare, *Julius Caesar*, Act III, Scene II.

ACKNOWLEDGMENTS

This section of the book was quite daunting to write. I mean how do I acknowledge all the people in my life who had a material impact? I don't think it is possible, and to those I do not mention, please accept my deepest thanks and apologies for the omission.

With that said, this is a relatively long chapter, as I have many people to thank for their direct and indirect help in understanding and enriching my life's journey and enabling me to write this book.

To my wife, Noelle, for your constant encouragement. You are an incredible writer with an uncanny sixth sense to know where to push a thought or when to drop it. You have urged me to write this book for years, and I finally listened. You and our precious rescue dog Velvet provide the perfect home environment for creative endeavors.

THE FOUNDATION

To my teammates from Little League Baseball to Pop Warner Football, to Junior High and High School Football, Lacrosse, and Wrestling, to Johns Hopkins Lacrosse, thank you for making me the best version of myself I could be. We had a blast, won a bunch of championships and always had each other's backs. I learned mental and physical toughness from you and the capacity to deal with adversity head on. The seeds for this book were planted on those playing fields.

My high school football and lacrosse coaches, Jack Salerno and Walt Sofsian, were two of the most influential people in my life. I spent four years learning about how to compete, how to be a good teammate and how to never offer up excuses for my shortcomings.

The Johns Hopkins lacrosse tradition of excellence is made possible by the caliber of its coaching staff. I was incredibly fortunate to play for Bob

Scott, Henry Ciccarone, Fred Smith, Jerry Schnydman, Joe Cowan, Willie Scroggs and Dennis Townsend. I learned a lifetime of invaluable lessons both on and off the field from arguably the greatest coaching staff in the history of the game.

Family and friends have been my rock since I was born. To the extent I had an edge in the competitive game of life, this was it. To my parents, may they rest in peace, who always encouraged me to be the best I could be, but never pushed me into anything I wasn't enthusiastic for. My brothers, Mitch and Steve, have always been there for me in every possible way—no questions asked. My niece Annie and nephews Zach and Max are all highly accomplished professionals, raising beautiful families. They are a source of immense pride. I have been close to my cousins my entire life, which has been a true blessing. Thank you cousins Sherri, Allan, Gayle, Larry K, Larry F, Nancy, Ellen, Bruce, Eleanor, Steven and Lynn. This family closeness includes the children and grandchildren of my parents' closest friends like the Loddengaard/Rubin clan.

I am truly blessed to remain close with numerous grammar school and high school classmates and teammates. There is nothing like old friends—no pretense, no peacocking—just memories of the most innocent and fun parts of our lives. Gene Small, Jeff Merrigan, Phil Quartuccio, Jerry Sigmund, Ron Cammaratta, Marshall Post, Mitchell Rosenberg, Robert Limmer and Gerry Fontano—you are truly brothers for life. To Lois Daly, thank you for always supporting me through every twist and turn in athletics and life.

Fraternity brothers (Beta Theta Pi) and others from Johns Hopkins remain intimate parts of my life. Dennis Gagamiros, Dr. Peter Schlossberg, Dr. Ira Fox, Dr. John Armitage, Dr. Howie Mandel, George Davis, Michael Moller and David Andrews (LSU, Stanford) are a source of continual wisdom and inspiration. Teammates from Hopkins lacrosse remain a special part of my life. Fellow freshmen on that epic 1974 NCAA championship team including George Johnson, Ritchie Hirsch, Tom Myrick, Bob Maimone and Kevin Mahon shared a unique bond that remains today. Senior captains of that team, Rick Kowalchuk and Jack Thomas, showed me what selfless leadership was all about. To all those Hopkins players from the 1970s and 1980s who go to the eastern shore of Delaware every summer, thank you for keeping us all young. Thank you fellow Blue Jays Frank Cutrone for organizing this year after year, Scott Baugher for memorializing these trips with epic photos and Phil Federico and Mark Greenberg for their gracious hospitality

THE PARTNERS AND PROFESSIONALS

To the partners who were instrumental in developing and fine tuning this book. Michael Levin was a true copilot on this journey, offering wisdom, sharp editorial direction, structure, encouragement, and lots of laughs as we developed this book. To the publishing team at Munn Avenue Press: Charlie Levin, Shannon Berning, Lily Drew, and designer Jess Marony. You truly believed in the vision of the book and exhibited extraordinary patience as we fine-tuned the manuscript and ensured all design elements were compelling and "on brand." I have already benefited from the sage advice of David Ratner at Ratner PR in navigating the complex media landscape of book marketing. Nick Bumgardner organized and pho-tographed the visuals in the book, adding essential depth to the story. Omelet's Senior Designer, Andre Cabral, was instrumental in refining the book cover design. Earnie Larossa and Steph Littleton from Johns Hopkins Athletics secured Hopkins lacrosse photos featured in the book from the Johns Hopkins archives; thank you so much for all you do. Elmont High School friend and classmate Mark Horowitz took many of the high school athletic pictures shown in the book; Mark you have always been a whiz behind the camera—thank you. A big thank you to Elmont Memorial High School who produced the Olympian yearbook from which a few photos were used in the book.

I reference legal issues in numerous sections of the book, and I want to acknowledge the friendship, excellent counsel and support from corporate and personal attorneys I have worked with including Peter Lauzon, Ryan Saba, Jonathan Kaufelt, Alan Epstein, Ronn Davids and Merrill Kraines. My long time accountant, Rick Marcus, has seen me through every up and down, always there with sound advice and empathy. Thank you Rick.

I am deeply fortunate to work with the most incredible team of professionals at Omelet. Our CEO Thas Naseemuddeen, CFO Naj Allana and CMO Sarah Ceglarski, have been my true partners for over ten years and are among the most capable and ethical people in the business world today.

In an industry rife with high turnover, we have benefited greatly from the dedication and loyalty of additional executives who have been with Omelet for 10 or more years including Melanie Simpson Rorie, Josh Smutko, Raul Montes, Jimmy Barker, Ricardo Diaz and Pete Talaba. Thank you to the rest of our outstanding Leadership Team, Chelsea Kauth, Zey McGlynn, Abba Binns. Florian Bodet and Sarah Donze. Ex-Omelet long-time executives Mike Wallen and Anna Nesser Hewson remain family and were instrumental in our success. Thank you to Omelet's founders Shervin Samari, Ryan Fey and Steven Amato who took a big risk to start Omelet over twenty years ago to revolutionize the advertising business. That revolution is very much alive today. A special shout out to Brandon Rooks, who, while emerging as a star producer, still manages Omelet's technology infrastructure and somehow solves every tech problem I have, bar none. This book would not have been completed without his ability to troubleshoot the myriad of technical problems I encountered throughout the writing process. Finally, thank you to my long time friend and Omelet board member Joe Boystak, for your sage counsel throughout the years. This unique Omelet team afforded me the time to focus on writing this book.

Thank you to my former colleagues around the globe at EMAK Worldwide. We built a phenomenal company together over a 25-plus-year period, forged lifelong friendships and had a blast along the way. Prior to my EMAK venture, I had been a management consultant for ten years. Three former colleagues, Steve Brauer, Kevin Welsh and Andy Zimmerman, have become life-long friends and confidants over the decades and provided inspiration for the book. Thank you and congratulations on your outstanding career successes.

Johns Hopkins University has had a profound influence on my life for 50 years. I entered as a cocky lacrosse player and exited with an appreciation of the world's beauty and complexity. As America's first research university, it has the highest of academic standards, but it has always been governed with remarkable humanity. I was honored to serve on the board of trustees during former president Bill Brody and current president Ron Daniels tenure—two truly extraordinary leaders who I learned a great deal from. Senior Vice President of Development and Alumni Relations, Fritz Schroeder, and Senior Vice President and Secretary of the Board of Trustees, Maureen Marsh, are two incredible professionals who keep me consistently connected to the university. Athletic Director Jen Baker and Head Men's Lacrosse Coach Peter Milliman ensure the Hopkins lacrosse tradition continues to thrive both on and off the field.

FAITH, HEALING AND RESILIENCE

Chapter 14 talks about the mind/body connection and the imperative of listening to your gut. To have a clear signal, you need to be mentally and physically healthy. I am fortunate to have care provided by some of the world's best health practitioners from the Vanderbilt University ecosystem, including Dr. William Sullivan, Dr. Byron Stephens, Dr. Aaron Yang, Dr. Charles Cox, Dr. Suneetha Amara, Dr. Arvindh Navaratnam Kanagasundram, and Dr. Stephen Schaaf along with RN Yolanda Heath and physical therapist Jill Porter. After my extensive spinal surgery, the incredible team of physical therapists at Elevate 615, including Brian Kaufman, Nate Stiffler, and Abby Daunis have enabled me to recover and resume my active lifestyle. Rabbi Yitzchok Tiechtel of Chabad of Nashville has been foundational in re-connecting with my Jewish faith and spirituality, and keeping life's many ups and downs in perspective.

THE PIVOT TO NASHVILLE

In 2020, while the pandemic was impacting all elements of work and personal life, Noelle and I decided to move from Los Angeles, which had been home for more than twenty years. A good friend and business associate Robert Hartman and his wife, Disney star Susan Egan, had recently moved from Southern California to Nashville and raved about it. As a singer/songwriter, Noelle was eager to visit Nashville and see if we liked it. My gut flashed a bright "go" and we ended up moving there in December, 2020. Thank you Robert and Susan for sharing the treasure of Nashville, TN. A big thank you to our neighbors and dear friends, the Cropper family (Angel, Steve, Andrea and Cameron), who literally adopted us as family from the moment we arrived in Nashville.

I quickly met a few other folks in town, and suddenly we had a core group of guys that became close friends. Almost every Tuesday night-going on five years now—we meet for dinner at an old-school Italian restaurant in Nashville, Valentino's, to talk about life. It is an incredible brotherhood. Thank you to Yosef , Kent, Wyn , Greg , Clarence, Brooke, Jason, Geoffrey, Jim and Alex. Family friendships, business deals and good old fashioned emotional support has emerged from our group. May we keep these dinners locked for decades to come. A heartfelt thank you to Karl and Corina, two Nashville confidants who help me navigate all of life's complexities.

While loving Nashville, I do miss Los Angeles—particularly some folks who have been close friends for decades. Bob Farina, Seth Glassman (Managing Partner at Gravitas, the incredible Beverly Hills private club), Tony High, Peter Adee, George Jones, Candy Schulman, Mark Matheny, and the entire Drago family—so many wonderful memories and no doubt many good times ahead.

Finally, to you the reader. Thank you for devoting your precious time to reading this book. I hope your life is somehow enhanced as a result.

ABOUT THE AUTHOR

Don Kurz is an entrepreneur, former championship athlete, and dance instructor. He has been a senior partner in a major international consulting firm, successfully taken a company public on Nasdaq, started a hedge fund, and currently is the executive board chair and principal shareholder of leading creative agency Omelet LLC.

Don served for twelve years on the Johns Hopkins University board of trustees and subsequently was elected a trustee emeritus for life. He was awarded the Johns Hopkins Heritage Award for exceptional lifelong service to the institution, and he has endowed the Kurz Family Scholarship to provide tuition support for low-income students.

He was a key player on the first Johns Hopkins University NCAA lacrosse championship team in 1974, though two serious knee injuries prematurely ended his lacrosse career in 1976. Don is currently an active mentor of student-athletes at Hopkins. He was voted the Outstanding Athlete at Elmont Memorial High School his senior year and has recently been inducted to the school's Athletic Hall of Fame.

Don was a dance instructor for Arthur Murray Dance Studios and was a regular at New York iconic disco Studio 54 in the late 1970s.

He earned his BA from Johns Hopkins University and an MBA from Columbia University.